Swim for the Health of It

Swim for the Health of It

Ernest W. Maglischo
California State College, Bakersfield

Cathy Ferguson Brennan
California State University, Long Beach

MAYFIELD PUBLISHING COMPANY
Palo Alto and London

10 9 8 7 6 5 4 3 2 1

Mayfield Publishing Company
285 Hamilton Avenue
Palo Alto, California 94301

Sponsoring editor: C. Lansing Hays
Manuscript editor: Linda Purrington
Managing editor: Pat Herbst
Production editor: Deborah Cogan
Art director: Nancy Sears
Designer (interior and cover): Al Burkhardt
Cover photograph: © Peeter Vilms/Jeroboam, Inc.
Illustrator: Mary Burkhardt
Production manager: Cathy Willkie
Compositor: Allservice Phototypesetting
Printer and binder: George Banta Company

To my wife Cheryl,

Ernie Maglischo

To my husband Larry,

Cathy Brennan

Contents

Part II   Stroke Mechanics

Part III   Triathlon

Preface

We wrote *Swim for the Health of It* as a text for intermediate, advanced, and conditioning classes that are taught in community and four-year colleges.

We are aware that short class periods, which usually last from 35 to 50 minutes, do not permit enough time for both instruction and conditioning. Assigning this text will allow you to reduce the amount of time spent in instruction. As a result, your students will have more in-class time to improve their aerobic fitness, and you will be able to give them more individual attention.

We have purposely discussed the technical information in this text in an informal and nontechnical style so that your students can understand and absorb the material quickly. And we have made extensive use of sequence photographs and illustrations in the sections dealing with stroke techniques, in order to eliminate long, complicated explanations.

The text is divided into three parts. We describe the training process in Part I (Chapters 1 through 5). We've devoted Part II (Chapters 6 through 8) to stroke mechanics. We discuss the rapidly growing sport of triathlon in Part III (Chapter 9).

Chapter 1 contains a description of the physiological and psychological benefits your students can expect to receive from engaging in a swimming conditioning course. Because you may have students new to the sport of swimming, we have provided information about what they'll need to know to get started. In Chapter 2, we describe important physiological principles of training, and in Chapter 3 we apply those principles to swim training. In Chapter 4 we suggest ways for students to evaluate their progress. In Chapter 5, we offer advice for dealing with common ailments and annoyances specific to swim training. The next three chapters are devoted to stroke mechanics: hydrodynamic principles of efficient swimming (Chapter 6); the four competitive strokes — front crawl, back crawl, breaststroke, and butterfly (Chapter 7); and the three most popular noncompetitive strokes — sidestroke, overarm sidestroke, and elementary backstroke (Chapter 8). In Chapter 9, we offer some advice for triathletes.

The material in this book is the result of our work over the years in teaching courses in swimming and conditioning. We believe *Swim for the Health of It* will be a useful supplement to your instruction and will help motivate your students to use swimming as a means of physical conditioning.

We are indebted to the many people who have helped prepare this book. We especially appreciate the assistance offered by the staff of Mayfield Publishing Company: C. Lansing Hays, Editor, for sponsoring this project; Pat Herbst, Managing Editor, for her guidance; Nancy Sears, Art Director, for her care in overseeing design and the preparation of the illustrations; and Deborah Cogan, Production Editor, for her careful attention to the project. Special thanks go to Manuscript Editor Linda Purrington for her many helpful suggestions. The design of the text is the result of the work of Al Burkhardt. We are indebted to him for the clear and orderly manner in which the text and illustrations are presented. The lifelike drawings are the work of Mary Burkhardt. They are, in our opinion, some of the best illustrations to appear in a swimming textbook. Special thanks also go to Larry Brennan, Vicki Johnson, and Julie Mayer for their editing, typing, and encouragement during the early stages of this project.

We would like to acknowledge the useful comments of the following swimming instructors and coaches who reviewed preliminary drafts of this text: Becky Binney, University of Texas at Austin; Richard Draper, University of Iowa; Glen Egstrom, University of California at Los Angeles; James R. Marett, Northern Illinois University; L. D. Newell, Baylor University; Candace Norton, University of Georgia; Jay Roelen, Saddleback College; and Valerie L. Turtle, University of Massachusetts.

We also want to thank everyone who participated in the filming sessions: T. R. Santos, Jill Symons, David Santos, Diane Braithwaite, Lorraine Rutthoff, Elizabeth Pavrel, Marsha Dahlgren, Tim Murphy, Mindi Bach, Matt Kowta, Kryston Peterson, and Kim Valentine.

Finally, we appreciate the students who have requested a book of this nature in order to further their exercise program through swimming.

Ernie Maglischo
Cathy Brennan

Swim for the Health of It

Introduction: Is This the Book for You?

We want to state at the outset that this is not a "learn to swim" book. We wrote it for people with a reasonable degree of proficiency who want to use swimming to improve their health and physical fitness. Our primary purpose was to provide a text that could be used in conjunction with the intermediate and advanced swimming classes that are taught in high schools, community colleges, and four-year colleges. However, we have also included information that can be used by people in other circumstances.

Having spent many years as swimming instructors, we understand the conflict that occurs when there is not enough time for training and instruction in a short, 35- to 50-minute class period. If you are enrolled in a swimming class, the information in these pages will reduce the amount of instruction you need so that you can spend more time training.

If you are a member of a "swim for fitness" group that does not provide instruction, this book may help you both to perfect your stroke mechanics and to understand the reasons behind the various workouts that you are asked to perform.

For competitive swimmers of any age, Chapters 2 and 7 briefly summarize the elements that are needed to succeed. If you compete in the rapidly growing sport of triathlon, the advice in Chapter 9 (and other chapters) may help you knock minutes off your swimming times.

Those of you who train alone may benefit most from our suggestions. We have stressed the "whys" as well as the "hows" of training so that you can plan training programs to meet your changing needs.

The only people who may not find this book immediately useful are nonswimmers. If you can't swim a length of the pool, enroll in a learn-to-swim class taught by a qualified instructor. When you can swim one or two lengths of the pool, you'll be ready to enjoy the benefits of swim training. Don't be stopped by the fact that your strokes aren't perfect. Perfect strokes — even average strokes — are not a prerequisite for swim training. If they were, very few of us would be able to use swimming — or, for that matter, any sport — as a vehicle for training.

We know that this book will be more valuable to you if the information can be absorbed and understood quickly so that you can spend a maximum amount of time training and a minimum amount of time reading. For this reason, we have discussed technical information in a nontechnical style, and we have made extensive use of sequence photographs and illustrations.

The text is divided into three sections. Part One, which comprises Chapters 1 through 5, describes the training process. Part Two, which includes Chapters 6 through 8, is devoted to stroke mechanics. In Part Three (Chapter 9) we offer some training advice to participants or potential participants in the sport of triathlon.

If the information in this book helps you in any small way to live a longer, happier, and more fulfilled life, we will have achieved our purpose.

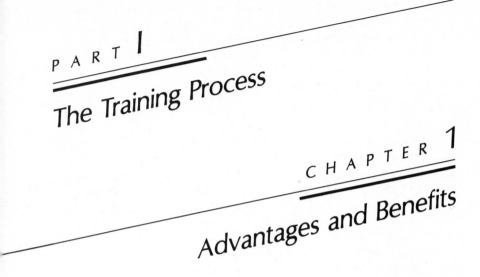

CHAPTER 1

Advantages and Benefits

People usually think of the terms *exercise* and *training* as synonymous. There is an important distinction between the two, however. The term *exercise* refers to the act of exerting oneself. Such exertion may be indiscriminate and may serve no purpose beyond enjoyment of the activity. On the other hand, *training* implies that you are exercising in a planned, systematic manner for the purpose of achieving certain goals.

This book was written for people who are serious about training. We have tried to provide you with all the information you will need to establish reasonable goals and to construct a training program that will accomplish those goals, regardless of your age or present swimming ability.

The Advantages of Swimming

You probably enjoy swimming and believe it is the best training medium for you. And you've made an excellent choice. Swimming is a superb form of exercise that will provide you with all the benefits you seek.

According to experts on health and fitness, the ideal form of training should meet the following criteria:

1. It should be continuous in nature and performed at a moderate pace that does not cause excessive stress and strain.
2. It should require the use of all or most major muscle groups in your body.
3. It should have a minimum of risk associated with participation.
4. It should be exhilarating and enjoyable.

Swimming satisfies these criteria more completely than any other form of exercise.

What are some of the advantages of swimming as a form of training? First, it requires the continuous use of more of your body's major muscle groups than do most other forms of exercise. Swimming is one of the few endurance sports that require vigorous use of the muscles of both the upper and lower body. The various armstrokes require contractions of the muscles of the arms, shoulders, chest, and upper back. Kicking conditions the muscles of the upper and lower legs, the gluteal muscles of the buttocks, the abdominal muscles, and the muscles of the lower back.

Second, swimming also provides a stimulus for muscle growth that is superior to most land activities of an endurance nature. Because it is 1,000 times more dense than air, water offers greater resistance to movement. The additional resistance encourages greater muscle growth. You need not worry about becoming too bulky, however. Muscle growth will be balanced by fat loss. Therefore, the size of most body parts—particularly your waist, hips, and thighs—will not increase. In fact, they'll probably be reduced because the rate of fat loss will exceed the rate of muscle growth.

Another advantage is that swimming requires the use of muscles on both the right and the left sides of your body. The result is a pleasing, symmetrical, muscular development. This is in stark contrast to most sports, particularly those where implements are used. Those sports tend to encourage greater muscular development on the dominant side of the body.

A very important advantage enjoyed by swimmers pertains to sports-related injuries. Swimmers are subject to fewer injuries than participants in practically any other sport. Many runners, for example, are being forced to abandon their sport because their knees and hip joints can't tolerate the constant pounding. Joint and muscle injuries are also common in racquet sports that require explosive applications of force. These sports place severe stress on the shoulders, elbows, knees, and hips.

Some swimmers suffer from inflammation of the shoulder and knee tendons. But those of you who swim for fitness, or even who compete in Masters competitions, will not be training hard enough to risk tendinitis.

Joint and muscle injuries are less prominent among swimmers because the water supports their bodies, thus alleviating the punishing and jarring effects of weight bearing. In addition, swimming movements are rhythmic and controlled, requiring no explosive applications of force. The absence of weight bearing and the nonexplosive nature of swimming movements makes this sport an ideal form of exercise for pregnant women and for people who are recovering from various joint and muscle injuries.

A last, very important advantage is that swimmers enjoy a reduced incidence of heat illness, because they dissipate body heat to the cool water. Thus they rarely suffer from heat exhaustion or heat stroke.

The Benefits of Swimming

Some of the appearance and circulatory benefits you can expect from just 8-12 weeks of swim training are listed in Table 1.1. The appearance benefits are body composition changes (increases in muscle tissue and decreases in body fat) and circumference changes (reductions in the size of body parts). The circulatory benefits include (1) decreases in heart rate, cholesterol, and blood pressure and (2) increases in stroke volume (the amount of blood pumped out of your heart with each beat).

TABLE 1.1
Training Benefits from Swimming

Physiological Measure	Training Benefit
Body composition changes	
Weight	loss: 2-6 lb
Fat	loss: 6-8 lb
Lean body weight (muscle)	increase: 2-4 lb
Circumference changes	
Waist	loss: 1-2 in
Hips	loss: 1-2 in
Thighs	loss: 1-2 in
Circulatory changes	
Resting heart rate	lower: 5-10 bpm
Working (submaximum) heart rate	lower: 10-12 bpm
Blood cholesterol	lower: 20-40 mg/100 ml of blood
Blood triglycerides	lower: 10-50 mg/100 ml of blood
Stroke volume	higher: 10-20 ml of blood
Blood pressure	lower: 8-20 mm Hg
HDL-C[a]	higher: 10-20 mg/100 ml of blood

[a]HDL-C stands for *high-density lipoproteins per 100 mg cholesterol*. The former help reduce the latter in human blood.
Source: Based on data from Adams, McHenry, and Bernauer, 1977; Doherty, 1977; Frick, Konttinen, and Sarajag, 1963; Luetkemeier, 1978; Wilmore, 1977.

Appearance Benefits

If you swim a minimum of 30–45 minutes per day for three to five days of every week, you can expect to lose between 2 and 6 pounds of body weight in approximately six weeks. This rather modest loss of weight underlies a more significant loss of body fat that will improve your appearance dramatically.

You will very likely add 2–4 pounds of muscle tissue to your arms, shoulders, chest, and legs while you are losing that 2–6 pounds of body weight. So you'll actually have lost 8–10 pounds of fat from your waist, hips, arms, and thighs. While the scale shows a loss of only 2–6 pounds of body weight, the actual loss of body fat will be considerably greater.

The significant loss of body fat coupled with the increase of muscle tissue that occurs with exercise will give your body a lean, firm, well-defined appearance that could not be achieved by dieting alone.

This shift in body composition will cause a reduction in the size of body parts where fat tends to be deposited in greatest amounts. In other areas of the body, fat loss may be offset by muscle growth so that there will be very little change in actual size. You can expect to reduce the circumference of your waist, hips and thighs by 1–3 inches, while other body parts will probably remain the same or will increase only slightly.

If you are overweight when you begin training, you can expect even greater losses. Overweight people must expend more calories than their normal-weight counterparts in order to perform the same amount of work; therefore, they tend to lose body fat at an accelerated rate. In one study, overweight female swimmers reported losses of 15–20 pounds of body weight during ten weeks of swim training. The circumferences of their waists and thighs were reduced 2–3 inches (Doherty, 1977). In another study, overweight middle-aged men lost 12–15 pounds of body fat during twelve weeks of swim training (Luetkemeier, 1978).

We advise you to have a qualified person calculate your body composition periodically by means of a skinfold test or by underwater weighing. Such measurements will allow you to recognize the true magnitude of fat losses and muscle tissue increases that have occurred. Realizing the extent to which you have improved can help you maintain your motivation for training.

Other Muscular and Skeletal Changes

In addition to increasing in size, your muscles will also become stronger and more enduring. The tendons that attach them to your bones will become thicker and tougher, reducing the probability of muscle tears and other stress-related injuries. Training also helps bones remain hard, strong, and resistant to fractures and chipping.

Improved Flexibility

Maintaining adequate flexibility lessens the likelihood of suffering back-aches and other joint pains, which are common among inactive people. Swimming can improve or maintain the range of motion in your joints, particularly in the lower back, hips, shoulders, and ankles. The correct execution of a wide variety of swimming strokes requires movements that act as stretching exercises for these joints. The repetitive recovery movements of the front crawl, back crawl, and butterfly strokes help maintain shoulder flexibility. The various kicks help maintain lower back, hip, and ankle flexibility. An adequate range of motion in these and other joints allows you to move smoothly and efficiently without fear of pain or injury.

Circulatory Benefits

As a swimmer, your heart will beat slower at rest and during exercise. It will also pump more blood to your muscles with each beat (an increased stroke volume). A greater blood supply with fewer heartbeats means a more efficient, and therefore healthier, circulatory system.

Stroke volume increases have been reported to exceed 10 to 20 ml after training. Reductions in resting and exercise heart rates of 10–20 beats per minute (bpm) have also been reported (Adams, McHenry, and Bernauer, 1977; Frick, Konttinen, and Sarajag, 1963).

Exercise encourages your blood vessels to remain flexible and elastic, so your blood pressure will stay within normal limits. Fatty materials (such as cholesterol) that can harden in these vessels, and can reduce or completely obstruct the flow of blood to critical organs of your body, are deposited less rapidly. The quantity of high-density lipoproteins (HDL) in your blood increases. HDL help eliminate fatty materials.

Reductions in blood pressure of 8–20 mm Hg have been reported after training. The quantities of fatty materials (cholesterol and triglycerides) have been reduced by 10–80 mg per 100 ml of blood, while the quantity of HDL has been increased by as much as 20 mg per 100 ml of blood (Wilmore, 1977; Woods, 1958). All these changes help maintain your blood pressure in the normal range or help reduce it to normal.

Why are these circulatory improvements important? First, they indicate that your circulatory system is more efficient and, therefore, more resistant to the heart and blood vessel disorders that are the leading causes of non-accidental deaths among the middle aged and elderly. When reductions in resting and exercise heart rates and increases in resting and exercise stroke volumes occur, they signal that your heart muscles have become stronger and more enduring and that your blood vessels are more elastic and free of hardened cholesterol. These improvements also signify an increase in the supply of oxygen and other nutrients to your muscles and organs.

Respiratory Benefits

You will find that training permits you to breathe more efficiently at rest and while exercising. You'll take slower, deeper breaths. No more embarrassing huffing and puffing that occurs when climbing stairs or hurrying to class and other appointments! These changes in respiratory rate and depth reflect an improved endurance of your respiratory muscles, an increased flexibility of your bronchial tubes, and an increase in usable lung space. If you maintain these improvements through middle age and later years, you'll have less chance of suffering from emphysema and other breathing disorders.

Psychological Benefits

The benefits of regular training are not restricted to physiological functions. Regular physical exercise almost always results in an improved self-image and a renewed zest for living. There is nothing like the total involvement and routine of physical exercise to reduce depressing thoughts. You'll feel more energetic and free from the embarrassing fatigue that comes from unexpected bursts of energy. You'll work at a faster pace. You'll be more alert, and you'll have energy for recreation after a long, hard day at work or school. You'll find you can relax more completely, you'll sleep better, and you'll require less sleep to feel refreshed. In short, you'll feel better about yourself, and when you feel that way about yourself others will enjoy your company more.

Getting Started

You may still have a few questions that need to be answered before you can start, such as "Where can I train?" and "What equipment will I need?" We'll answer those questions in this section.

Where Can You Train?

Where can you train? In a pool, obviously. But which pool, when, and with whom? If you are enrolled in a swimming class, those problems are solved. If you are not, your local high school, community college, or university probably has a pool that provides recreational swimming hours for students and community members. If no high school or other institution in your city has a swimming pool, undoubtedly a community pool provides time for recreational swimming.

You needn't be concerned that these pools will be too crowded for training. Most pools provide lanes for lap swimming during their recreational hours, and you'll be able to train in those lanes without interference from swimmers who are horsing around or cooling off.

If you prefer to train with a group, you'll find that most communities provide that opportunity through clubs and fitness groups. Local U.S. swimming teams often have Masters swimming programs where you can train under the supervision of a coach. Don't feel intimidated if you have never been a competitive swimmer. Although these teams include many former interscholastic and intercollegiate competitors who are now competing as adults, fast swimming is not the primary purpose of such programs. They are structured, first and foremost, to provide opportunities for adults to improve their fitness. Training programs are designed for every level of ability within these groups. Participation on a Masters team can be pleasurable and rewarding. Masters swimming involves competition for adults against others in their age group. The age groups are 25-29, 30-35, and so on in 5-year increments. There are people competing in the 85-90 age group and even some registered swimmers beyond the age of 90. You'll appreciate the guidance offered by experienced swimming coaches, and you'll enjoy the camaraderie of dedicated exercisers.

What You'll Need

Swimming is an inexpensive sport, requiring only $12-$25 to get started. You'll need a swimming suit and a pair of swimming goggles. We recommend a nylon or lycra racing suit. Many good brands are manufactured by reputable companies, and you can find them at any sporting goods store. These suits are vastly superior to the baggy cotton types that are sold in most clothing stores. They fit skin tight so that you encounter less resistance when you swim. They dry quickly, and if washed after each use they'll last a year or two without losing their shape.

Swimming goggles improve vision and reduce eye irritation. Some popular styles are shown in Figure 1.1. The chemicals used to maintain sanitary pool water may irritate your eyes; swimming goggles will keep the water out of your eyes. They also allow you to see where you are going underwater. You'll swim in a straight line, and you'll avoid collisions with other swimmers. You'll also be more able to judge your turns, and you'll be more aware of your arm and leg movements. In short, you'll enjoy swimming more when you can see what you're doing.

Your goggles may occasionally become fogged. You can prevent this by using one of several defogging solutions that are on the market. These products can usually be purchased at scuba diving supply shops and at some sporting goods stores. Saliva is also an excellent defogging solution. A few drops of saliva spread over the inside of the lenses will keep your

Figure 1.1. Swimming goggles

goggles clear during an entire workout. And most major swim supply companies are now selling antifog goggles. These goggles have specially treated lenses that really do resist fogging.

If you have never used swim goggles, you will probably curse us the first time you try them. They'll leak, they may become fogged (if they are not an antifog type), and they'll slip off. You'll think they are impossible to swim with. But don't throw them away in disgust. Using goggles requires a period of adjustment. After a week you'll learn how to remedy these problems, and you'll never want to swim without goggles again.

Don't Forget a Physical Examination

You should have a thorough physical examination before you begin your training program. This is for your own safety. The doctor will be able to advise you concerning your capacity for exercise, and that advice will allow you to feel more secure in your efforts once you begin training. Be sure to choose a physician who is interested in and knowledgeable about training. Some physicians (although fewer now than a decade ago) still think exertion can be harmful for anyone over age thirty. Most, however, realize that training, when prescribed properly, will improve health. Ask the supervisor of the pool where you plan to train to suggest a physician. He or she will usually recommend someone who is active and interested in exercise. Don't overlook the importance of a physical examination in your desire to get started.

CHAPTER 2

Some Principles of Training

The purpose of this chapter is to acquaint you with some important principles of training. Understanding these principles will help you to train in the most effective manner. The first part of this chapter discusses principles concerned with the frequency, intensity, and time of training. The second part describes the most common method of swim training; namely, interval training.

F. I. T.

The three most commonly asked questions about training are

1. How many days per week should I train (frequency)?
2. How hard should I train (intensity)?
3. How long should I train (time)?

You can remember these three elements of training easily by thinking of them as the abbreviation *F.I.T.*

Your answers to these questions will, of course, depend on the time you have available for training. Therefore, we'll keep the usual time constraints of a busy person in mind as we discuss each of these elements. We'll cite minimum and maximum standards for each that will allow you to construct a program that fits your particular schedule. We'll begin with a discussion of training frequency.

Frequency

One day of exercise per week is better than none, and you can attain noticeable improvements in appearance and aerobic fitness by training twice a week. But the best results are obtained when you train four or five days per week. After training for four or five days of each week, you reach a point of diminishing returns. That is, training more frequently will not improve your results in proportion to the additional time spent. Noncompetitors usually find that the small amount of additional improvement is not worth the time and effort required to produce it.

With regard to weight loss, it is obvious that you will burn more calories, and thus lose weight at a faster rate, if you train six or seven days per week. If losing weight is your goal, you may want to train more frequently than four or five days per week. Once you have reached your desired body weight (or your desired body composition), you can "cut back" to four or five days per week and concentrate on health and aerobic fitness.

Intensity

Perhaps the most important principle involved in improving your physical condition is that you must exercise at rates that are intense enough to *overload* your body's physiological systems. An overload is achieved when you train at more intense rates than your normal daily activities. Taxing your muscles, heart, and lungs thus stimulates improved strength, endurance, and flexibility.

One error in judgment that training enthusiasts make, perhaps more than any other, is that they believe merely "putting in time" will provide the health and appearance benefits they seek. They train at a slow pace that is no more intense than casual strolling and then wonder why they don't look and feel better. *You must overload to improve.*

How do you translate this abstract notion of overload into specific measures that will tell if you're training properly? The four most effective measures of training intensity available are:

1. Counting your heart rate immediately after each swim
2. Timing each swim
3. Noting your breathing rate after each swim
4. Monitoring your feelings of effort while you swim

Heart Rate. For healthy adults, an exercise heart rate between 120 and 170 bpm is considered adequate for aerobic fitness training. How do you count your heart rate while you're swimming? You don't. You can estimate your exercise heart rate by counting your pulse rate for six seconds immediately after each swim. Add a zero to this count, and you will have your approximate exercise heart rate per minute.

You can use this method with confidence because your pulse will not have slowed to any appreciable extent in only six seconds. Therefore, the minute figure that you calculate will be very close to your true exercise rate.

The easiest site for counting your immediate postexercise heart rate is at your carotid artery. Don't try to count the beats at your wrist. They are more easily counted at your neck when your heart is beating fast and hard. The swimmer in Figure 2.1 is shown counting her heart rate at the carotid artery.

A heart rate of 120 bpm indicates the minimum swimming speed that will improve your physical condition. Swimming at speeds that elicit 140-170 bpm will provide even greater improvements. On the other hand, it is neither necessary nor advisable to train at heart rates higher than 170 bpm because swims at this intensity are primarily supported by anaerobic rather than aerobic metabolism. Why is aerobic metabolism superior to anaerobic for training? A discussion of these two phases of metabolism is in order here.

Exercise that relies predominantly on aerobic metabolism is moderate in

Figure 2.1. Counting heart rate

intensity and continuous or nearly so in nature. Aerobic exercise is the type that will improve your health and fitness most. It reduces fat deposits and creates a demand for additional oxygen that your body meets through improved functioning of your heart, lungs, and muscles.

There is an optimum intensity of aerobic training that will produce the best results. Training below this intensity will cause inferior results. Training above this intensity will also produce inferior results. Exercise that is too intense relies predominantly on anaerobic metabolism. Anaerobic metabolism provides a fast source of energy for sustained sprints, but it also produces the waste product lactic acid, which, in turn, lowers the pH of body tissues, causing pain and discomfort in the process. Anaerobic exercise is essential for training competitive athletes who push themselves to the limits of their endurance in order to win contests. However, it does not produce any of the physiological adaptations that improve health, fitness, and appearance, and therefore is not a necessary ingredient of most fitness programs.

Swimming Speed. After you have been training for a while, it is a good idea to complete some time trials in order to determine how fast you can swim some of the repeat distances that you use frequently in training. You can then estimate your proper training intensity by swimming at certain percentages of these "all out" efforts.

The proper intensity for aerobic training is somewhere between 75 and 90 percent of your maximum speed for a particular distance. More intense swims of 90–100 percent are primarily anaerobic and do not improve the aerobic training effect. The calculations in Figure 2.2 may help you understand what we mean by the term "percent effort." It depicts a method for calculating an 80 percent effort for 100-yard repeats. The hypothetical swimmer in this illustration has a best time of 70 seconds for 100 yards of freestyle. To calculate an 80 percent effort, subtract 80 percent from 100 percent and multiply the remainder times 70 seconds. Then add that figure to 70 seconds to determine your proper training speed.

Figure 2.2. Calculating percent efforts

100% − 80% = 20% or .20

70 sec + 14.0 sec = 84.0 sec

For this hypothetical swimmer, an 80 percent effort for a set of 100-yard freestyle repeats would be 84.0 seconds per 100 yards swum.

Swimming Effort Scale

10	All out	Ideal for improving
9	Nearly all out	anaerobic endurance
8		Ideal range for improving
7	Moderately hard	aerobic endurance
6	Moderate	
5		
4	Easy	Too slow for training.
3		Suitable only for warming up
2		
1	Very easy	

Figure 2.3. Swimming effort scale

Breathing Rate. Swimming your practice repeats at the proper speed will result in a breathing rate that is considerably faster than normal when you finish each swim. You should not be heaving and gasping for breath, but you should be breathing at least twice as fast as you would normally breathe at rest. An immediate postrepeat breathing rate of three or four breaths in 5 seconds usually indicates the proper aerobic training speed.

This method is less exact than the two means of monitoring training intensity described earlier. Nevertheless, it is convenient and, if the guideline is followed, is effective.

Feelings of Effort. The least exact, but most commonly used method for monitoring training intensity is to estimate how hard you are working by the sensations of effort that you feel. Exercise physiologists refer to this method as "rating your perceived exertion." The proper training speed is one that makes you feel that you are working at approximately three-quarters effort during your repeats. That intensity can be maintained for long periods of time and is sufficient to produce training effects.

An easy way to use perceived exertion for monitoring your training intensity is to rate your effort on a scale of 1 to 10 (see Figure 2.3). A rating of 7 or 8 is ideal for aerobic fitness training.

Time

Before discussing the optimum length of time for training, we should state clearly that exercising for any length of time, even 5 minutes per day, is better than no exercise at all. However, to make significant improvements you should train for 30–60 minutes per day. This amount of daily exercise significantly reduces the degenerative effects of aging and inactivity that normally occur in our circulatory, respiratory, muscular, and skeletal systems.

Unfortunately, researchers have not been able to determine whether longer is better once the minimum daily training requirement of 30–60 minutes has been met. If you have the desire and the time to train for longer periods of time, do so. Don't expect your results to increase in direct proportion to the time spent, however.

After you have been training for a while, you'll probably begin judging the duration of your workouts in terms of the number of yards you swim per day rather than the number of minutes you spend training. If you prefer this method and you are an experienced swimmer, you should be able to complete 2,000–4,000 yards in 30–60 minutes. Less experienced swimmers can probably cover 1,000–3,000 yards in the same time.

Swimmers who judge their training time by yardage should not be concerned if they are swimming fewer yards than their partners are during a training session. Your training benefits are determined by the amount of time you spend working, not by the number of yards you swim. An inexperienced swimmer who completes 1,000 yards in 30 minutes receives the same training stimulus as an experienced swimmer who covers 2,000 yards in the same time.

By the way, don't try to swim as many yards as possible during your first few weeks of training. Allow yourself plenty of rest between sets of repeats during your early training sessions. After two or three weeks, you should gradually reduce the amount of time you spend resting and increase the amount of time you spend swimming. Some guidelines for determining the amounts of time you should spend swimming and resting are presented in the next section, on interval training.

Interval Training

The term *interval training* is used to describe the system of multiple repeat swims used by most swim training enthusiasts. An example of a typical interval training repeat set is to swim ten 100-yard swims at 75–90 percent effort, with approximately 30 seconds of rest between each swim. This set of repeats can be written as follows:

Interval training sets contain four variables:

1. The *number* of repeats (10, in the example given)
2. The *distance* of each repeat (100 yards)
3. The *rest interval* between each repeat (30 seconds)
4. The *speed* of each swim (75-90 percent of their best time for the repeat distance). This could also be stated in terms of
   - a heart rate of 140-170 bpm
   - a breathing rate of four breaths in 5 seconds
   - a feeling of working at 75 percent effort
   - a perceived exertion rating of 7 or 8 on a scale of 10

The best results are achieved with certain combinations of these variables. Some suggestions concerning these combinations are offered in the following sections.

Distance of Each Repeat

Aerobic fitness can be improved by repeats of any distance, if completed at the proper intensity. It's boring to swim the same repeat distances each day. The usual repeat distances for swim training are 50 yards/meters (swimming pools are usually 25 meters or 50 meters, in length), 100 yards/meters, 150 yards/meters, 200 yards/meters, 300 yards/meters, 400 yards/meters, 500 yards/meters, 800 yards/meters, and 1,000 yards/meters. In a short-course pool (25 yards in length), each 50-yard repeat is equal to two lengths of the pool. One hundred yards is equal to four lengths, and so on. In long-course pools (50 meters in length), each 50-meter repeat is one length of the pool, while a 100-meter repeat is two lengths, and so forth.

Number of Repeats per Set

One important guideline should be applied to the number of repeats per set: the minimum number should provide an adequate aerobic overload. To achieve this overload, we recommend that each repeat set be a minimum of 10 minutes long, including both swimming and resting time. Approximately 3-5 minutes of work are required to get all the physiological mechanisms involved in aerobic metabolism operating near peak efficiency. Therefore, 10 minutes should provide enough time to mobilize and overload these mechanisms.

Don't misunderstand what we have just said. We are not suggesting that you train for only 10 minutes per day. We are recommending that each of your repeat sets should require a minimum of 10 minutes to complete. You should do *several* such sets in a workout.

The optimum number of repeats per set is not known. Let your motivation and the time you have available for training guide your choices after you've met the 10-minute minimum. Some suggestions are listed in Table 2.1. These suggestions are given for highly skilled, good, and novice swimmers. For purposes of definition, a *highly skilled swimmer* has had previous competitive experience or swims as well as most ex-competitive swimmers. *Good swimmers* are proficient in a variety of swimming strokes and con-

TABLE 2.1
Some Suggestions for Constructing Effective Repeat Sets

Repeat Distances	Highly Skilled Swimmers		Good Swimmers		Novice Swimmers	
	Number	Departure Time[a]	Number	Departure Time[a]	Number	Departure Time[a]
50	10–20 in sets of 10 or more	0:45–1:00	8–15 in sets of 5 or more	1:00–1:30	8–10 in sets of 3 or more	1:30–2:00
75	10–12 in sets of 8 or more	1:15–1:30	8–10 in sets of 6 or more	1:30–1:45	6–8 in sets of 3 or more	2:30–3:30
100	8–12 in sets of 5 or more	1:30–1:45	6–10 in sets of 4 or more	2:00–2:30	5–8 in sets of 2 or more	3:00–4:30
150	5–8 in sets of 4 or more	2:15–2:30	4–6 in sets of 3 or more	2:30–3:30	3–5 in sets of 2 or more	4:30–6:30
200	4–6 in sets of 5 or more	2:45–3:00	3–4 in sets of 2 or more	4:00–6:00	2–4 in sets of 1 or more	6:00–8:00
300	3–4	4:00–4:30	2–3	5:30–6:30	1–2	10:00–13:00
400	2–4	5:30–6:00	1–3	7:00–9:00	1–2	12:00–17:00
500	2–3	6:30–7:30	1–2	9:00–11:00	1	16:00–25:00

[a]The departure times are given as the number of minutes:seconds, from the beginning of a repeat to the beginning of the next swim.

sider themselves above average in this respect. *Novice swimmers* have just begun training and do not feel their swimming ability is quite up to average. Serious trainers do not remain novices for very long.

Rest Intervals Between Repeats

The most significant improvements in aerobic endurance are achieved when the rest periods between swims are less than one-half the time required to complete the swim. This relationship is expressed as a work:rest ratio of 2:1. Other, even more effective work:rest ratios are 3:1, 4:1, and 5:1. You may use even less rest in relation to work time for the longer repeat distances (400 meters and longer).

Short rest periods improve aerobic fitness more effectively than longer rest periods because they don't allow the swimmers enough time to recover between repeats. The most effective aerobic fitness training occurs when swimmers begin the next repeat with their breathing and heart rates still considerably elevated from the previous swim. This condition causes their physiological systems to remain overloaded for the entire set of repeats, including both the rest periods and the work periods. If they rested until these systems were nearly recovered, they would spend a considerable amount of each training session operating below the proper training intensity. This would, of course, reduce the training effect. A good rule of thumb is to start the next repeat while you are still breathing faster and deeper than normal if you are using your breathing rate to monitor training intensity. If you are using your heart rate for that purpose, you should start the next repeat before it has dropped below 130 bpm. We've suggested some appropriate rest intervals for the most commonly used repeat distances in Table 2.2.

You may be wondering why you should rest at all. After all, the best way to prevent recovery would be to swim continuously for long periods of time. Although this is certainly an effective way to train for aerobic fit-

TABLE 2.2
Suggested Rest Intervals for Popular Repeat Distances

Distance	Rest Interval
25 yd	5–10 sec
50 yd/m	10–20 sec
75–100 yd/m	10–45 sec
150–200 yd/m	20 sec–1 min
300–400 yd/m	1–3 min approximately
400 yd/m and longer	1–3 min approximately

ness, most swimmers would complain of boredom if it were the only type of training that they used. You probably don't need to be told that boredom is one of the most serious deterrents to training. Most people prefer to train with a variety of repeat distances, including both long and shorter swims. Since both methods provide the benefits you seek, use them both to keep your training sessions interesting and motivating.

The rest intervals listed in Table 2.2 indicate the optimum amount of rest that swimmers should take between repeats of certain distances. However, when you train with a group, you'll find it simpler to plan your rest intervals in terms of departure times rather than rest intervals. The use of departure times allows workouts to proceed in a more orderly manner.

When several people are swimming their repeats at different speeds in the same lane, operating on rest intervals would cause them to start their repeats at widely varying times. Inevitably, some would be ready to start a repeat when others were attempting to turn at the same end, and the swimmers would collide and generally get in each other's way. Using departure times reduces congestion because swimmers start each repeat in close sequence and can swim in single file down one side of the lane and back on the other. We'll describe this single-file traffic pattern in greater detail in the next chapter.

An example of a set of repeats on departure times would be to swim ten 100-yard repeats, leaving every two minutes (10 × 100 yd/2 min). Let's assume that the various swimmers in the pool need between 1:20 seconds and 1:40 seconds to complete each 100-yard swim. Some swimmers will get 40 seconds of rest between each swim while others will get only 20 seconds. Should this be a matter of concern? The answer is no. When the departure times are set properly, as is the case here, all the swimmers in the lane will be working at an effective work:rest ratio. The faster swimmers in the previous example would be operating on a work:rest ratio of 2:1 (80 seconds of work and 40 seconds of rest), while the slower swimmers have a ratio of 5:1 (100 seconds of work and 20 seconds of rest). Both ratios are adequate for aerobic fitness training. Some suggested departure times were listed with the repeat sets in Table 2.1. These departure times were also listed according to ability.

If you find that you do not fit one of the categories listed in Table 2.1, you can determine your best departure time for a particular repeat distance by using the following method. Swim the repeat distance at an effort that feels right for training. Check your heart rate or breathing rate at the end of the swim to make certain you were swimming at the proper speed. Then note the time of the swim. Add 5–60 seconds to that time, depending on the work:rest ratio you prefer, and use that sum as your departure time. If this should result in an unusual departure time, such as 1:51.0, round the time up or down to the nearest 15-second interval (see Figure 2.4).

Suppose you swam 100 yards of freestyle in 1:21, and you wish to use a 30-second rest interval.

1:21.0 + 30 sec = 1:51.0

This interval may be rounded downward to 1:45.0 or upward to 2:00.0.

Figure 2.4. Determining departure times

The consistency of your repeats will provide an indication of the adequacy of the departure times you've selected. You are consistent when you are able to swim all the repeats in a set at nearly the same speed. For example, suppose you decide to swim ten 100-yard repeats on a 1:45.0 interval. If you can swim all those repeats at approximately 1:20.0, you are consistent. However, you are obviously inconsistent if you swim the first 100-yard repeat in 1:20.0 and the second in 1:30.0, with each of the eight remaining swims becoming progressively slower. Inconsistency indicates that the departure time is too difficult. In such cases, it would be better to swim the repeats on a longer departure time. For example, the same work:rest ratio can be maintained if the set of 100 repeats in question was swum on a 2-minute departure time at an average speed of 1:30 to 1:40 seconds.

Your departure times should be reduced as you get in better condition. You will know when it is time to reduce your departure times because your repeats will get faster and/or feel easier to swim.

CHAPTER 3

Training Procedures

Now it's time to put the principles of the preceding chapter into practice. This chapter provides some concrete suggestions on how to construct your day-to-day training program. We also discuss some common training procedures in this chapter. You need to know these procedures in order to train effectively. We also discuss some controversial practices. Like all other sports, swimming has some unique training procedures that are valuable, some that are not so valuable, and others whose value has not been determined. We'll give you our recommendations when we feel an opinion is justified.

Constructing Your Daily Training Program

Our goal in Chapter 2 was to educate you concerning the training process so that you could select and combine various repeat sets to suit your particular needs. We've included some sample training schedules in the tables on the following pages to help you in this respect. You'll notice that we have studiously avoided the approach of listing exactly what repeats you should swim on Monday, Tuesday, and so on, throughout the week. We don't want to take all the fun and creativity out of training. We have, instead, presented the workouts in a "smorgasbord" form that will allow you to "mix and match" the sets according to your needs and mood. The repeat sets are designed for the three ability levels defined earlier. Repeat sets for novice swimmers are listed in Chart 3.1. Sets for good swimmers are listed in Chart 3.2, and some suggestions for highly skilled swimmers are listed in Chart 3.3.

CHART 3.1 *Training Sets*
for Novice
Swimmers

Note: The numbers in parentheses indicate departure times for strokes other than front crawl.

1. WARM-UP

A. Swim 100 yd/m easy, any style.
B. Swim 50 yd/m. Kick 50 yd/m, easy.
C. Swim 50 yd/m. Pull 50 yd/m, easy.
D. Swim 50 yd. Swim 3 × 25 yd on 1 min.

2. MAIN SWIMMING SETS

A. Swim 500 yd/m front crawl.
B. Swim 2 × 300 yd/m front crawl on 9 min (10 min).
C. Swim 4 × 200 yd/m front crawl on 6 min (7 min).
D. Swim 6 × 100 yd/m front crawl on 3 min (4 min).
E. Swim 12 × 50 yd/m front crawl on 1:30 (2 min).
F. Swim 10 × 75 yd/m front crawl on 2:30 (3 min).
G. Swim 2 × 200 yd/m front crawl on 6 min (7 min).
   Swim 2 × 100 yd/m front crawl on 3 min (4 min).
   Swim 4 × 50 yd/m front crawl on 1:30 (2 min).
H. Swim 50, 100, 200, 100, and 50 yd/m any style or combination of styles. Take 30-sec rest between each swim.
I. Swim 300, 200, 100, and 50 yd/m any style or combination of styles. Take 30-sec rest between each swim.

3. KICKING SETS

A. Kick 150–200 yd/m any style.
B. Kick 2 × 75 yd any style on 3 min.
C. Kick 100 yd/m any style on 4 min. Then kick 50 yd/m.
D. Kick 4 × 50 yd/m any style on 1:30.
E. Kick 6 × 25 yd on 1 min.
F. Kick 1 × 100 yd any style on 4 min. Then kick 4 × 25 yd/m on 1 min.
G. Kick 2 × 50 yd any style on 1:30. Then kick 4 × 25 yd on 1 min.

---

4. PULLING SETS

A. Pull 200 yd/m any style.
B. Pull 150 yd/m on 4:30 (5 min). Then pull 50 yd/m.
C. Pull 2 × 100 yd/m front crawl on 3 min (4 min).
D. Pull 3 × 75 yd front crawl on 2:30 (3 min).
E. Pull 4 × 50 yd/m front crawl on 1:30 (2 min).
F. Pull 100 yd/m front crawl on 3 min (4 min), then pull 2 × 50 yd/m front crawl on 1:30 (2 min).
G. Pull 8 × 25 yd any style on 45 sec.
H. Pull 100 yd on 3 min, then pull 4 × 25 yd on 45 sec.
I. Pull 25, 50, 75, 50, and 25 yd any style or combination of styles. Take 15-sec rest between each swim.
J. Pull 50, 100, 100, and 50 yd/m any style or combination of styles. Take 30-sec rest between each swim.

---

5. SPRINT SETS

A. Swim 6 × 25 yd any style on 1 min.
B. Swim 3 × 50 yd/m any style on 2 min.
C. Swim 1 × 50 yd on 2 min, then 2 × 25 yd on 1 min.

---

6. COOL-DOWN

A. Swim 100–200 yd/m any style, easy.
B. Swim 100 yd/m and kick 100 yd/m, easy.

CHART 3.2 *Training Sets for Good Swimmers*

Note: The times in parentheses indicate departure times for strokes other than front crawl. Individual medley means divided among butterfly, back crawl, breaststroke, and front crawl.

1. WARM-UP

A. Swim 150–200 yd/m, easy.
B. Swim 100 yd/m. Kick 100 yd/m.
C. Swim 100 yd/m. Pull 100 yd/m.
D. Swim 100 yd. Then swim 3 × 25 yd on 45 sec.

2. MAIN SWIMMING SETS

A. Swim 800–1,000 yd/m front crawl.
B. Swim 2 × 500 yd/m front crawl on 9 min (10 min).
C. Swim 2 × 400 yd/m front crawl on 7:30 (9 min).
D. Swim 3 × 300 yd/m front crawl on 6 min (7 min).
E. Swim 5 × 200 yd/m front crawl on 3:30 (4 min).
F. Swim 6 × 150 yd/m front crawl on 2:45 (3 min).
G. Swim 8 × 100 yd/m front crawl on 2:15 (2:30).
H. Swim 10 × 75 yd front crawl on 1:45 (2 min).
I. Swim 15 × 50 yd/m front crawl on 1:15 (1:30).
J. Swim 400, 300, 200, and 100 yd/m any style or combination of styles. Rest 30 sec between each swim.
K. Swim 50, 100, 150, 200, 150, 100, and 50 yd/m any style or combination of styles. Rest 15 sec between each swim.
L. Swim 1 × 400 yd/m front crawl on 7:30.
Swim 2 × 200 yd/m front crawl on 3:30.
Swim 4 × 100 yd/m front crawl on 2:15.
M. Swim 2 × 200 yd/m front crawl on 3:30.
Swim 4 × 100 yd/m front crawl on 2:15.
Swim 8 × 50 yd/m front crawl on 1:30.
N. Swim 2 × 25, 50, 75, 100, 75, 50, and 25 yd any style or combination of styles. Take 15-sec rest between each swim.
O. Swim 4 × 200 yd/m individual medley on 5 min.
P. Swim 8 × 100 yd individual medley on 2:30.
Q. Swim 2 × 200 yd individual medley on 5 min.
Swim 4 × 100 yd individual medley on 2:30.

3. KICKING SETS

A. Kick 200 yd/m
B. Kick 150, 100, and 50 yd/m. Take 15-sec rest between each repeat.
C. Kick 2 × 100 yd/m on 2:30.
D. Kick 3 × 75 yd on 1:45.
E. Kick 4 × 50 yd/m on 1:20.
F. Kick 1 × 100 yd on 2:30.
   Kick 2 × 50 yd/m on 1:45.
G. Kick 8 × 25 yd on 45 secs.
H. Kick 2 × 50 yd on 1:45.
   Kick 4 × 25 yd on 45 secs.

---

4. PULLING SETS

A. Pull 200–300 yd/m.
B. Pull 2 × 200 yd/m front crawl on 3:30 (4 min).
C. Pull 2 × 150 yd/m front crawl on 2:45 (3 min).
D. Pull 3 × 100 yd/m front crawl on 2:15 (2:30).
E. Pull 4 × 75 yd front crawl on 1:45 (2 min).
F. Pull 5 × 50 yd/m front crawl on 1:15 (1:30).
G. Pull 200 yd/m front crawl on 3:30 (4 min), then 100 yd/m on 2:15 (2:30).
H. Pull 50, 100, 100, and 50 yd/m. Take 15-sec rest between each swim.
I. Pull 25, 50, 75, 100, 75, 50, and 25 yd any style or combination of styles. Take 15-sec rest between each swim.
J. Pull 1 × 100 yd/m front crawl on 2:15 (2:30 for m).
K. Pull 25, 50, 75, 100, 75, 50, and 25 yd any style or combination of styles. Take 15-sec rest between each swim.
L. Pull 1 × 100 yd/m front crawl on 2:15 (2:30).
   Pull 2 × 50 yd/m front crawl on 1:15 (1:30).

---

5. SPRINT SETS

A. Swim 8 × 25 yd/45 sec any style.
B. Swim 4 × 50 yd/1:30 any style.
C. Swim 1 × 50 yd/1:30 any style.
   Swim 4 × 25 yd/45 sec any style.

---

6. COOL-DOWN

A. Swim 100–200 yd/m, easy. Use any style or combination of styles.

B. Kick 100 yd/m, easy.

CHART 3.3 *Training Sets
for Highly Skilled
Swimmers*

Note: Departure times are listed in ranges because of the wide range of speeds encompassed by this category. The numbers in parentheses indicate departure times for strokes other than front crawl.

1. WARM-UP

A. Swim 200–300 yd/m, easy.

B. Swim 200 yd/m. Then kick 100 yd/m.

C. Swim 200 yd/m. Then pull 100 yd/m.

D. Swim 200 yd/m. Then swim 3 × 50 yd/m on 1 min.

2. MAIN SWIMMING SETS

A. Swim 1,500–2,000 yd/m of front crawl.

B. Swim 2 × 800 yd/m front crawl on 12–14 min (14–16 min).

C. Swim 3 × 500 yd front crawl on 7–8 min (8–10 min).

D. Swim 3 × 400 yd/m front crawl on 5–7 min (6–8 min).

E. Swim 4 × 300 yd/m front crawl on 4–6 min (5–7 min).

F. Swim 6 × 200 yd/m front crawl on 3 to 3:30 (3:30 to 4 min).

G. Swim 8 × 150 yd/m front crawl on 2:15 to 2:30 (2:30 to 3 min).

H. Swim 10–12 × 100 yd/m front crawl on 1:30 to 2 min (1:45 to 2:30).

I. Swim 12–14 × 75 yd front crawl on 1:15 to 1:30 (1:20 to 1:40).

J. Swim 20 × 50 yd/m front crawl on 45 sec to 1 min (1 to 1:15).

K. Swim 800 yd/m front crawl on 12–14 min.
   4 × 200 yd/m on 3:00 to 3:30 (3:30 to 4 min), or
   6 × 150 yd/m on 2:15 to 2:30 (2:30 to 3 min), or
   8 × 100 yd/m on 1:30 to 2 min (1:45 to 2:30).

L. Swim 400 yd/m on 5–7 min.
   Swim 2 × 200 yd/m on 3 to 3:30 (3:30 to 4 min).
   Swim 4 × 100 yd/m on 1:30 to 2 min (1:45 to 2:30).

M. Swim 400 yd/m on 5-7 min.
  Swim 2 × 200 yd/m on 3:00 to 3:30 (3:30 to 4 min).
  Swim 8 × 50 yd/m on 45 sec to 1 min (1:00 to 1:15).
N. Swim 2 × 200 yd/m front crawl on 3:00 to 3:30 (3:30 to 4 min).
  Swim 4 × 100 yd/m front crawl on 1:30 to 2 min (1:45 to 2:30).
  Swim 8 × 50 yd/m front crawl on 45 sec to 1 min (1:00 to 1:15).
O. Swim 100, 200, 300, 400, 300, 200, and 100 yd/m, using any style or
  combination of styles. Rest for 15-30 sec between each swim.
P. Swim 500, 400, 300, 200, 100 yd/m, using any style or combination of
  styles. Rest 15-30 sec between swims.
Q. Swim 5 × 200 yd/m individual medley on 3:00 to 3:45.
R. Swim 10 × 100 yd individual medley on 1:45 to 2:15.
S. Swim 400 yd individual medley.
  Swim 2 × 200 yd individual medley. Rest 15-30 sec between swims.
  Swim 4 × 100 yd individual medley.

3. KICKING SETS

A. Kick 200-300 yd/m.
B. Kick 3 × 100 yd/m on 2:15 to 2:30.
C. Kick 4 × 75 yd on 1:45.
D. Kick 5 × 50 yd/m on 1 to 1:15.
E. Kick 8 × 25 yd on 1 min.
F. Kick 200, 100, and 50 yd/m. Rest 10-20 sec between each repeat.
G. Kick 50, 100, 100, and 50 yd/m. Rest 10-20 sec between
  each repeat.
H. Kick 100, 75, 50, and 25 yd. Rest 10-15 sec between each repeat.
I. Kick 200 yd/m, then kick 4 × 50 yd/m on 1 to 1:15.
J. Kick 3 × 50 yd on 1 to 1:15.
  Kick 6 × 25 yd on 45 sec.
K. Kick 2 × 100 yd/m on 2:15 to 2:30.
  Kick 4 × 50 yd/m on 1 to 1:15.
L. Kick 200 yd/m. Rest 30 sec.
  Then kick 2 × 100 yd/m on 2:15 to 2:30.

4. PULLING SETS

A. Pull 300-400 yd/m.
B. Pull 2 or 3 × 200 yd/m front crawl on 3:00 to 3:30 (3:30 to 4 min).
C. Pull 3 or 4 × 100 yd/m front crawl on 1:30 to 2 min (2:00 to 2:30).

D. Pull 6 × 50 yd/m front crawl on 45 sec to 1 min (1:00 to 1:15).
E. Pull 200 yd/m, rest 30 sec.
   Then, pull 4 × 50 yd/m on 45 sec to 1 min (1:00 to 1:15).
F. Pull 50, 100, 100, and 50 yd/m. Rest 10–15 sec between each repeat.
G. Pull 100, 75, 50, and 25 yd/m. Rest 10–15 sec between each repeat.

---

5. SPRINT SETS

A. Swim 10 × 25 yd on 30 sec.
B. Swim 5 × 50 yd/m on 1 min.
C. Swim 2 × 50 yd on 1 min.
   Swim 6 × 25 yd on 30 sec.

---

6. COOL-DOWN

A. Swim 200–300 yd/m, easy.
B. Swim 200 yd/m. Then kick 100 yd/m.

A typical daily training session should include the following elements, which should be completed in the sequence described:

1. *Stretching*. Spend three to five minutes stretching the joints of your shoulders, back, groin, and ankles before entering the water. We describe some good stretching exercises at the end of this chapter. Practice them for two to three minutes.
2. *Warm-up*. Spend two to three minutes warming up in the water. The best procedure is to swim 100–300 yards/meters with an easy long stroke. This prepares your body physically. In the meantime, you can prepare yourself mentally by thinking about the types of repeat sets that you are going to do. Some warm-up swims are suggested in Column 1 of Charts 3.1, 3.2, and 3.3.
3. Select a *main series* of repeats from Column 2. This will be a set of repeats designed to improve aerobic fitness. The series should be done on short rest, and it should require 10–30 minutes to complete.
4. Select a *kicking set* from Column 3.
5. If there is time remaining, you may wish to include another set of repeats. This may be a *pulling set* from Column 4, a *sprint set* from Column 5, or another aerobic set of repeats from Column 2. For variety, you may want to swim this final set using a stroke different from the one you used in the main series.

6. *Cool down* with another easy swim of 100–300 yards/meters. Some suggestions are provided in Column 6. Cooling down encourages the rapid removal of waste products and prevents blood from pooling in your extremities. You'll recover from your workout in a shorter time, and you'll feel better later in the day if you take the time to cool down.

Please heed the following advice before you start training. Do not use interval training right away. Interval training is effective, but it is also a strenuous way to train. Be sure you are ready for it. Swim easy for a few days (or weeks) until you can complete 400 meters or 500 yards without stopping. Then you can train with intervals without fear of strain.

What If Your Time Is Limited?

Most of us have approximately 45 minutes to an hour available for training each day. Therefore, the previous suggestions were based on that time frame. If you have more time available, you can lengthen some repeat sets, or you can add some sets. However, on some days the time available for training may be 30 minutes or less. In such cases, the best advice we can give you is to eliminate kicking, sprinting, and pulling and to swim the entire workout using either (1) long straight swims or (2) sets of shorter repeats on very short rest intervals. We offer this advice because kicking and pulling reduce the total muscular involvement per session as compared to swimming the full stroke. When your time is limited, you gain more benefits by exercising as many muscle groups as possible for as long as possible during the training session.

It would also be advisable to swim your repeats at a slightly faster rate of speed. With time at a premium, an increase in training speed can, to some extent, substitute for reduced quantity. You'll also burn more calories. This does not mean that you should sprint the entire workout. It simply means that you should swim most of your repeats near the high end of the measures for aerobic training intensity that were recommended in Chapter 2; that is, at heart rates of 150–170 bpm or with a breathing frequency of five breaths per 5 seconds. If you are gauging your training intensity by repeat speeds, you should be swimming at 85–90 percent effort. A perceived exertion rating of 8 or 9 would also indicate the proper intensity.

Using the Pace Clock

Once you have constructed your daily training program, you will need a method for timing your repeats and determining your departure times.

Figure 3.1. Pace clock

The large clock with the sweep second hand is used for that purpose. It is called a *pace clock.* Pace clocks are usually found sitting on the deck or mounted on a wall at one or both ends of the pool (see Figure 3.1).

You may have some difficulty reading the pace clock at first. However, it is a rather simple skill to master. Let us say that you wish to swim a set of 50-yard repeats on a one-minute departure time. You would push off the wall at the end of the pool as the second hand (usually the red hand) passes the 60-second mark. Swim 50 yards, and look at the clock immediately as you finish. It will tell you (1) how fast you swam the repeat and (2) the amount of time remaining until your next 50-yard swim. Suppose, for example, that it took you 45 seconds to swim the 50-yard repeat. You would get 15 seconds of rest before starting the next repeat.

That was a simple departure time because each repeat began at 60 seconds. Here's an example of a more difficult departure time. Suppose you were swimming 50-yard repeats on a 1:05 departure time. Suppose also that your time for the first repeat was 45 seconds, once again. You would get 20 seconds of rest after the first repeat, and you would start the second repeat as the second hand passes the 5-second mark. If you swam the second repeat at the same speed, the second hand would be on 50 seconds when you finished (45 seconds to swim the repeat plus the 5 seconds that you left after the 60-second mark). With 20 seconds of rest, the third repeat would begin as the second hand passed the 10-second mark. Each succeeding repeat would start 5 seconds later than the preceding swim.

Traffic Patterns

Due to the increasing popularity of swim training, it will usually be necessary to share your lane with two or more people. Under these circumstances, it is essential that certain "traffic patterns" be established and that each swimmer train courteously and obey the "rules of the road." Just as with highway driving, certain traffic patterns and rules of the road are in common use in swimming pools. If you know these rules, you can fit into any training situation.

The traffic pattern is quite simple when only two people are swimming in a lane. One person can swim back and forth on the right side while the other swims on the left side. This "sides" pattern eliminates the need for passing and allows swimmers the freedom to swim different strokes and to use different repeat distances and departure times when training.

Swimming in a lane with several other people requires a different organization. The most common traffic pattern is to swim single file in a counterclockwise circle. This method is called, for obvious reasons, a circle pattern.

The swimmers should start their repeats 5 or 10 seconds apart, with the fastest swimmer in the lane going first, the second-fastest going second, and so forth. Keep your eyes open, and stay on your side of the lane to avoid collisions. When you wish to pass someone, tap him or her on the foot and wait until he or she reaches the wall before you attempt the pass. The swimmer who is being passed should stop at the wall and allow you to pass. Don't be one of those swimmers who speeds up or crowds the center of the lane when someone attempts to pass.

Traffic flows more smoothly when all the people in the lane are doing the same repeat set on the same departure time. Swimmers who kick when others are trying to swim always get in the way of the faster-moving group. Likewise, the lane always becomes congested if someone is swimming one of the slower strokes while others are swimming the front crawl stroke.

Kicking: Is It Good for You?

Those red, blue, and yellow pieces of styrofoam you've seen lying around the pool are called *kickboards*. They are used to condition your legs

Figure 3.2. Kickboard

and to improve your kicking skill. Kickboards are held in the manner shown in Figure 3.2. Kicking also provides a rest for your arms while you continue to improve the endurance of your heart and lungs. It is a good idea to include at least 200–500 yards/meters of kicking in your daily workouts.

What About Pulling?

Those white cylindrical pieces of styrofoam are called pull-buoys. They are used to keep your legs afloat so that you can swim without kicking. This procedure, called *pulling,* permits you to isolate and overload your arms. Pull-buoys should be placed between your thighs as shown in Figure 3.3.

Pulling drills can also be performed with small black innertubes placed around your ankles in a figure-eight pattern (see Figure 3.4). These "pulling tubes" increase resistance to forward motion and thus overload your arms considerably more than they are overloaded by the pull-buoys.

Which are more effective for pulling drills, pull-buoys or pulling tubes? Some prefer the pull-buoys because they float your legs in a natural position. Others prefer pulling tubes because they provide greater resistance.

We prefer pull-buoys over pulling tubes, because we feel they encourage the use of more efficient stroke mechanics. Pulling tubes may cause your legs to be held in an unnaturally high position (if overfilled) or an un-

Figure 3.3. Pull-buoy

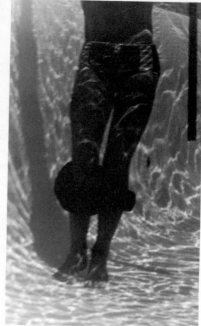

Figure 3.4. Pulling tube

naturally low position (if underfilled). This change of body position may, in turn, cause you to stroke in a less efficient manner. The lesser resistance of pull-buoys, as compared to pulling tubes, can be compensated for by swimming faster.

Hand Paddles: Do They Work?

You've undoubtedly noticed swimmers wearing pieces of plastic on their hands. These are called *hand paddles*. The swimmer in Figure 3.5 is wearing a pair of hand paddles.

Hand paddles are believed to serve two major purposes. First, they are supposed to improve your armstroke by guiding your hands and arms into the correct stroking patterns. Although this belief is widely held among competitive swimmers and coaches, it has been neither proven nor disproven by research.

Another supposed benefit of hand paddles is that they increase strok-

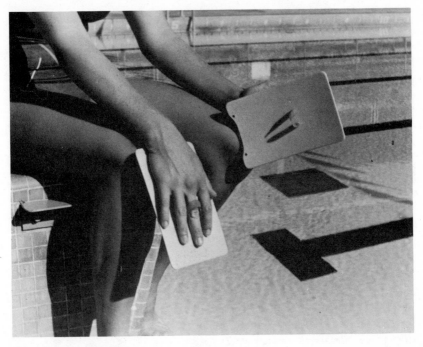

Figure 3.5. Hand paddle

ing force. The broad, flat surface of the paddles increases the resistance of the water to the swimmers' stroking efforts and is believed to thus provide a form of in-water resistance training that increases the strength and endurance of the stroking muscles.

We do not recommend hand paddles. We doubt that they provide enough resistance to increase stroking force to any appreciable extent. More importantly, some experts believe they contribute to tendinitis in the shoulder area (Anderson, 1976). Nevertheless, we realize that some of you will use hand paddles despite our advice. If you are one of those people, please discontinue their use at the first sign of shoulder pain.

Other Pulling Devices

Swimmers also use a variety of other in-water resistance training devices. There are kickboards that have a flat frontal surface that increases resistance as you kick forward through the water. Some swimmers wear

Figure 3.6. Drag suit

"drag suits," a belt with pockets that catch water and increase resistance to forward motion (see Figure 3.6). Still others wear weights on their hands to increase resistance (see Figure 3.7).

It is doubtful that any of these items will improve your training results. They cause you to work against more resistance but usually at a slower rate, so that there is little if any increase in work performed. On the other hand, they may produce subtle changes in your stroke mechanics that will, in time, reduce your efficiency. We advise against using them.

Figure 3.7. Wrist weights

Figure 3.8. Fins for kicking

Swim Fins Do Help

Swim fins are another popular training aid (see Figure 3.8). We endorse their use, particularly for swimmers with weak kicks. Kicking with fins may improve your kick by increasing your ankle flexibility. In addition, their use makes it possible to complete the kicking portion of your workouts at a faster rate of speed. This allows you to do more total work per session.

Fins are also an excellent training aid for novice swimmers. Inexperienced swimmers frequently become exhausted after the first few minutes of training because they lack the skill to swim efficiently. Swim fins reduce the effort required to swim and allow swimmers to train longer without becoming exhausted. In time, the additional yardage will improve their endurance and their swimming skill. After that they will no longer need the fins (except for occasional kicking drills).

Of course, fins can be overused. Be sure to do a sizable portion of your kicking without fins so that you maintain a feel for the water.

The Pros and Cons of Other Training Procedures

Competitive swimmers and coaches have developed a number of specialized training procedures. Some of these can improve your training effects under certain circumstances, while the value of others is questionable.

The purpose of this section is to acquaint you with some of the most popular procedures and also to discuss their value to the noncompetitor. The first of these is sprinting.

Should You Sprint?

Sprinting is fun. Most of us like to challenge ourselves occasionally by swimming short distances at top speed. It adds variety to our training. However, it will not improve our health to any appreciable extent.

Sprinting is an anaerobic activity and does not produce the health-improving adaptations of the respiratory, circulatory, and muscular systems that were mentioned in Chapter 1. If you were forced to make a choice between sprinting and swimming that would improve aerobic fitness, you should choose the latter. The aerobic swimming will improve your health, while the sprints will only increase your speed.

Luckily, most of us have enough time available for training, and we are not forced to make this choice. Therefore, if you like to sprint and you have the time to add 200–500 yards/meters of this type of swimming to your workout, feel free to do so.

The advice given in the last paragraph is for noncompetitive swimmers. Those who swim in Masters competition *must* make time for sprinting. Racing demands a high degree of speed and anaerobic endurance as well as a considerable amount of aerobic endurance. The former two capacities are developed by fast swimming. Therefore, sprinting should be included in your training program. We want to caution you about overdoing it, however: don't let your desire to win races cause you to lose sight of the most important reason for training; that is, to maintain good health. The desire to perform well in competition can be quite seductive. If you are racing in short events, you may be tempted to reduce your aerobic yardage and to spend a great deal of your time sprinting. Resist that temptation and be sure to include an adequate amount of aerobic endurance swimming in your training sessions.

What About Land Resistance Training?

Over the years, competitive swimmers have used several forms of land resistance training to improve their strength and swimming speed. Some of the more popular systems have been weight training, Universal Gyms, Nautilus training equipment, Mini Gyms, Biokinetic Swim Benches, and surgical tubing. We have already indicated that speed should not be a concern for noncompetitors. Does this mean that noncompetitors cannot benefit from land resistance training? Certainly not. The major benefit that noncompetitors receive from this form of training is an increased rate of muscle growth. This, in turn, provides a more firm appearance for women and a more muscular appearance for men. (Research has shown that resistance training does not cause the muscles of women to increase to the same extent as those of men — Wilmore, 1974.) If muscle growth is a goal of yours, you should include some land resistance training in your program. Any good book on resistance training can give you the information you need. Several are listed at the end of this book.

A subsidiary, and often overlooked, benefit of resistance training is that the resulting increase in muscle mass will increase your metabolic rate. As a result you can consume a few more calories, possibly 50–100 more per day, without increasing body fat. This may not seem a significant benefit unless you realize that being able to consume an additional 100 calories per day without gaining weight prevents a 10-pound weight gain each year. In addition, you will be less hungry and will not need to go through each day yearning for food.

Our advice concerning land resistance training would be the same as the advice we offered concerning sprinting. Include some resistance training in your program if you have the time and the inclination. However, don't neglect your aerobic fitness training to do so.

Is Hypoxic Training Helpful?

In recent years, hypoxic training (reducing the frequency of breathing) has become a popular part of many swim programs. When training hypoxically, swimmers breathe only once during every second, third, or even every fourth arm cycle. This is in contrast to the normal procedure of breathing once every arm cycle. The explanation that has been offered for the value of hypoxic training is that breathing less frequently will increase the intensity of the work, enabling swimmers to achieve the same training effects without swimming as far or as fast.

The argument in favor of hypoxic training sounds logical. Nevertheless, the value of this procedure has not been substantiated by research. In fact, the available research indicates that it is no more effective for improving aerobic fitness than swimming your practice lengths with unrestricted breathing (Craig, 1979; Dicker, Lofthus, Thornton, and Brooks, 1980).

Should You Stretch?

The stroking efficiency of some swimmers is reduced by tightness (restricted motion) in the joints of their shoulders, lower backs, hips, and ankles. For such people, stretching exercises, such as those pictured in Figure 3.9, can improve the range of motion in those joints.

Figure 3.9. Stretching exercises

Figure 3.9. (continued)

Figure 3.9. (continued)

Stretching exercises are also an excellent warm-up procedure. They loosen your muscles and joints and prepare them for effort while reducing the probability of injury. Most of the exercises shown in Figure 3.9 can be performed in or out of the water. They may be done slowly and rhythmically, or as a held-stretch procedure, with or without a partner.

The relative merits of the various methods of stretching—ballistic, held, and partnered—are not discussed here. Any of the three methods will increase the range of motion in your joints. A discussion of the advantages and disadvantages of each can be found in Suggested Readings 5, 7, 8, or 9, which are listed at the end of this book.

We do, however, want to give you a word of caution about stretching. Some orthopedic surgeons and trainers are now warning against the use of partner stretching and, indeed, against any type of flexibility exercises where people try to push their limbs and trunk beyond the normal range of motion. There is the possibility that excessive stretch—that is, forcing joints well beyond their normal range of motion—will injure the soft tissues and articulations around those joints. If you use stretching exercises, use them cautiously. Stretch only to the point of tightness. *Do not force joints beyond this point.* You will be able to extend your range of motion as the joints loosen.

CHAPTER 4

Evaluation and Motivation

You should include some form of evaluation in your training program so you will have a record of the improvements you've made. Improvement is one of the most powerful motivators. When you can see that you are swimming better, your desire to train will remain high. The purpose of this chapter is to describe some methods for evaluating your progress and for maintaining a high level of motivation for training.

Evaluating Your Progress

Evaluation should be an ongoing process. You should evaluate what you've done after each workout, and you should consider ways in which you can improve the next training session. One of the best ways to do so is by keeping a log.

The Swimmer's Log

Many swimmers evaluate their progress through the use of a daily training log. Some of these are quite extensive. They include

1. The total distance swum
2. The various repeat sets that were swum, including departure times
3. The average speeds for the various repeat sets or listings of some other method for determining intensity
4. Immediate postrepeat heart rates
5. Recovery heart rates

These records are usually annotated with subjective statements that describe the swimmers' feelings about the workout and their plans for future workouts. Logs often show such statements as "My backstroke feels off, I think I'll work on it tomorrow" or "I need more middle-distance swims on short rest tomorrow." Some sample log sheets can be found in Appendix A. You may want to use these until you establish your own log book.

Improving Your Repeat Times

The average time for your repeat sets is, perhaps, the most convenient indicator of improvements in aerobic fitness. When you find yourself consistently swimming your 100-yard repeats at an average speed of, for example, 1:30.0 rather than 1:40.0, you can be certain that your aerobic endurance has improved and that you are gaining all the health, fitness, and appearance benefits that were mentioned in Chapter 1.

Other Evaluation Procedures

It is also a good idea to have some periodic self-testing procedures to help you evaluate your progress. For this purpose, we suggest (1) distance swims for time and (2) heart rate counting. In addition, body weight, girth measurements, and, if possible, a body composition test are good indicators of fat loss and muscle growth.

Distance Swims for Time. A good test of aerobic fitness is to swim 400–800 meters or 500–1,000 yards for time. Distances of 400 meters or 500 yards are suggested for novices, while distances of 800 meters or 1,000 yards are ideal for good swimmers and highly skilled swimmers.

These distances require aerobic swimming. Therefore, when you have lowered your time you can be sure that your aerobic fitness has improved. We recommend that you select one of these distances for self-testing and swim it for time every two or three weeks. Record the time in your log and compare it to earlier times as the months go by. You'll be surprised at the improvements you'll make. Some norms are listed for 500- and 1,000-yard swims in Table 4.1. They are derived from the records of college swim classes that included both male and female swimmers of varying abilities. These figures are presented so that you can determine your standing relative to other swimmers of similar ability.

TABLE 4.1
Distance Swimming Norms

Ability Category	Percentile of Swimmers	500-yard Swim	1,000-yard Swim
Highly skilled swimmers	90	6:15	12:30
	80	7:30	15:00
Good swimmers	70	8:30	17:30
	60	9:30	20:00
	50	11:00	22:30
Novice swimmers	40	12:00	25:00
	30	13:30	27:30
	20	14:30	30:00
	10	16:00	32:30

Heart Rate Counting. We mentioned the value of your heart rate as an indicator of training intensity in Chapter 2. Two other aspects of heart rate counting can be used for evaluating your training progress: (1) reductions in resting heart rate and (2) the faster recovery of your heart rate to normal after exercise. The following suggestions can help you use resting and recovery heart rates to evaluate training progress.

It is well known that your resting heart rate drops as your aerobic fitness improves. The reduced rate signifies that your heart is putting out more blood with each beat, which in turn indicates a very healthy improvement of circulatory function. The technical term for this improvement is an increase in *stroke volume.*

In order to get an accurate measurement of your resting heart rate, count your heartbeats immediately on waking and before getting out of bed. Count your pulse at the carotid artery, as described in Chapter 2. Take a 30-second count, and multiply the number that you get by 2 to compute your minute rate. Record this figure for future comparison.

If you wonder how your resting heart rate compares to the average, you should understand that there is no such thing as an "average" resting heart rate. A "normal" resting rate can be identified within a wide range, however. Healthy people may have normal resting heart rates that vary from 30 to 80 bpm. There is no truth to the belief that well-trained athletes should have resting rates of 30–40 bpm. Some athletes do have resting rates in this range; however, there are others who are equally well conditioned with resting rates of 70–80 bpm. Don't be concerned if your resting heart rate is higher or lower than the rates of some of your friends. The important indicator of an improvement in aerobic fitness is that your resting heart rate declines as you progress through your training program.

We indicated in Chapter 2 that your heart should be beating between 130 and 170 bpm immediately after the last repeat of a set. In well-conditioned people, that rate drops quite rapidly during the rest period that follows. People who are not so well conditioned need a longer recovery period (assuming work of equal duration and intensity). Therefore, you should expect your heart rate to recover toward normal in a shorter time as your aerobic fitness improves.

Don't expect your heart rate to recover to resting during the recovery period, at least not during the first few months of training. Initially, it should drop toward 100 bpm within three minutes of recovery time. After training for a month or two, you will find that it recovers below 100 bpm after only two minutes of rest. Later, only one minute of rest may be required to produce the same reduction.

The best procedure for counting your recovery heart rate is to take three 15-second counts during the rest period following a main series of repeats. Take the first count one minute after completing the set; take the second count two minutes after finishing; and take the third count three minutes after. Convert each count to a minute rate, and record them in your log. Do this at least once each week and watch yourself recover faster as your fitness improves.

The decline in resting and recovery heart rates will be rapid in the early weeks and months of training. However, you should expect a plateau after awhile. It may then take several weeks before you notice another decrease.

The Scale and the Tape Measure. Recording and comparing your body weight and certain body circumferences from time to time will make you aware of the changes in body composition that have resulted from your training. Your motivation is bound to remain high when you realize just how many pounds and inches you have lost.

The procedure for determining your body weight does not require any explanation. You are probably aware, however, that all scales are not equally accurate. Therefore, be sure to weigh yourself on the same scale whenever possible. Also, try to weigh yourself at the same time every day, to reduce the interference of such factors as (1) the length of time between meals and (2) daily variations in water retention.

Girth measurements should be taken on each side of your body with a reliable tape measure made of a nonstretch material. Measure the circumference of the following body parts: upper arms, chest, waist, hips, thighs, and calves. In every case, take the measurement around the widest area of the body part in question. Keep the tape level. There is a form for recording your measurements in Appendix B. Over the weeks, you should see reductions and, in some cases, increases in the circumferences of these body parts that are of the magnitude indicated in Chapter 1.

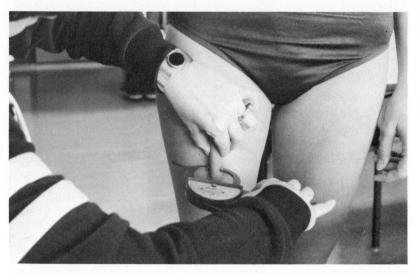

Figure 4.1. Skinfold measurement

Skinfold Tests: A More Accurate Way to Measure Body Composition. In the hands of a qualified person, skinfold calipers can provide a very accurate estimate of the percentage of your body weight that is made up of fat tissue and the percentage that is lean tissue. The skinfold calipers are used to measure the thickness of a fold of skin at various sites on your body. The photograph in Figure 4.1 shows a swimmer having a skinfold measurement taken at the thigh. The fold of skin and subcutaneous fat is pinched between the jaws of the calipers, and a reading is taken in millimeters. A fold of skin would normally measure approximately 3 mm. Therefore, measurements that are larger than 3 mm indicate the presence of fat. Of course, the larger the measurements become, the more fat you have deposited beneath your skin.

These measurements are taken at several sites on the body where fat is generally deposited in greatest amounts. The results are inserted, together with your body weight, into a standardized formula from which it is possible to calculate the percentage of your body weight that is made up of fat.

Unfortunately, skinfold tests are not completely accurate; they are only estimates of body composition. However, the various procedures and formulas that are used have been validated against more accurate but also more complicated and time-consuming methods. Therefore, if your skinfold test has been administered by a competent professional, you can feel confident that the results are within 1 to 2 percent of your actual percentage of body fat. You can find a competent professional to administer a skinfold test at most fitness centers and community college or university physical education departments. The test should not be expensive. It is painless and requires only a few minutes to administer.

Here is some information that can help you evaluate your results. In the average female, approximately 25 percent of her body weight is made up of fat tissue. The average male is 15 percent body fat. Those figures can help you determine how much weight you need to lose in order to have average body composition. If you wish to be below average, you should establish the following as your goals. Most well-trained female fitness enthusiasts have body fat percentages in the range of 18–22 percent. Most well-trained men have body fat percentages that are in the neighborhood of 8–12 percent.

Skinfold tests can serve another important function. They can help you estimate the extent to which you have increased the amount of muscle tissue in your body. The percentage of your body weight *that is not fat* consists primarily of bone, muscle, fluid, and air. For obvious reasons, this figure is commonly known as *lean body weight.* Muscle is the only one of these constituents that is likely to increase with training. Therefore, if your body fat percentage decreases out of proportion to your weight loss, you can be certain that muscle growth has occurred. For example, suppose that a person weighed 150 pounds with 15 percent body fat before starting training. This means that his or her lean body weight totaled 127.5 pounds while the remaining 22.5 pounds was composed of fat tissue (.15 × 150 = 22.5 pounds). Let's suppose further that after one month of training that body weight has been reduced to 145 pounds and that the body fat has decreased to 10 percent. Given these figures, the swimmer would have lost 8 pounds of body fat, and muscle tissue would have increased by a total of 3 pounds (.10 × 145 = 14.5 pounds).

Motivating Yourself to Train

If you thought that the first chapter of this book sounded like an advertisement for exercise in general and for swimming in particular, you were correct. Our purpose was to motivate you to train until you derived the benefits you seek.

Make a Commitment

A certain amount of commitment to training is necessary in the early weeks. The first three weeks are usually the most difficult. That is because it is too soon to see results, and the painful realization that their exercise tolerance is dramatically reduced (from their teenage and early adult years) causes many well-intentioned people to become discouraged.

We suggest that you make a pact to continue training for six to eight weeks, no matter what. If you train conscientiously for that length of time, you'll look and feel so much better that you'll probably continue training for the rest of your life. Your improvements will become noticeable, and you'll be surprised how closely your performances approximate the "good old days." In fact, if you've never trained seriously until now, you may find that you're in the best shape of your life and these will become the "good new days."

Set Goals

Setting goals can help maintain your commitment to regular training. These goals should be challenging but achievable. Don't set unrealistically high goals. You may become discouraged if you do not achieve them when, in reality, you are making excellent progress. By the way, setting unrealistically high goals is sometimes a subconscious way to avoid commitment. People who set impossible goals sometimes find it easier to give up because "The goal was unachievable anyway."

Don't set goals that are unrealistically low, either. When goals are too easy to achieve they lose their power to motivate.

Your first goal should be to "stick it out" for eight weeks. "Sticking it out" does not mean that you won't miss a workout occasionally. There are bound to be occasional unexpected circumstances that interfere with your training plans. Expect to miss a workout once in a while, but don't allow these disruptions to discourage you or cause you to give up.

Your next goals should concern the frequency and duration of your workouts. How many days per week will you train, and how many minutes per day will you swim? If you are a busy student or a working person, you probably find it difficult to train more often than three to five days per week or for more than 30–50 minutes per session. This may seem insufficient when compared to the time that athletes spend in training. However, you can take comfort in the fact, proven by research, that these combinations of frequency and duration are adequate for health and fitness purposes.

After you've been training for a few weeks, you may want to stimulate your interest further by setting some performance goals. For example, you may decide that you should complete a certain number of yards per workout. You may try to swim your repeats faster than previously. You may also decide to take less rest between practice swims. Perhaps you may want to do some sprinting, or you may wish to swim some time trials. These are all effective ways to motivate yourself and make your training more enjoyable.

Remember that your rate of improvement will usually increase in direct proportion to your motivation and enjoyment for training.

The information in Chapter 2 will help you set performance goals. If you need some additional advice, you can undoubtedly find a competent swimming instructor or coach around the pool. These people are usually dedicated, enthusiastic teachers who are eager to help. Don't be afraid to ask them for advice.

Maintain Interest

Lastly, we want to mention the problem of boredom in training. Some people like the regimentation, and they do not mind swimming the same repeats day after day. Others detest repetition. If you are in the latter category, be sure to include lots of variety in your training.

There are many ways to prevent boredom. One is to save a favorite drill for the end of the session. This will give you something to anticipate as you complete less preferred swims. It is often helpful to change strokes during a workout. Alternate your favorite stroke with a less preferred stroke. You can also add variety by alternating a kicking or pulling set with a swimming set. Other minor adjustments that can keep your training from becoming boring are to occasionally change the time and the length of your workouts. A change of scenery also can help: change lanes occasionally, and take opportunities to swim in different pools.

Writing out a plan for your workouts one week in advance may help maintain your motivation for training. The weekly plan becomes a sequence of daily goals that prompts you to train regularly. Include combinations of (1) challenging days and (2) days that are more relaxed. You should also include combinations of challenging sets and more relaxed sets within a single workout. Contrary to popular belief, most people enjoy rather than avoid occasional challenges. Only when the challenges become too frequent or impossible to achieve do they lose their power to motivate. This is when it becomes important to include some relaxation in your training. A relaxed day or set offers a nice change of pace and renews enthusiasm for the next challenge.

Training with a friend or with a group of friends is another excellent way to maintain enthusiasm for training. You'll look forward to the visits with your friends at practice. You'll enjoy the conversation before and after the workout and during the rest periods between repeats. And you'll also enjoy the fact that swimming with friends improves your training speeds. Friendly competition is a powerful motivator. Perhaps most importantly, swimming with friends promotes a sense of responsibility that will get you to practice even on days when you feel "down."

Often adding some "fun drills" to your program offers a change of pace from a traditional swimming workout. Here are some suggestions:

Life-Saving Stroke. Swim head up front crawl with flutter kick 25 yards. It is also fun to swim 15 yards head up front crawl, then swim the last 10 yards with head in the regular front crawl position. (This drill can be incorporated into the sprint portion of the workout.)

Changing Direction Swim. Start swimming head up front crawl. When the instructor blows the whistle, change directions and swim regular front crawl until the whistle blows again. The instructor can vary the length of time between whistles.

Ascending/Descending Yardage Workout. Start with a 50-yard swim. Then swim 100-, 200-, 400-, 500-, 400-, 200-, 100-, 50-yard swims. Rest 15–30 seconds between each swim.

Interchanging Stroke Swim. This drill can be used in sprints or the distance portion of the workout. Use front crawl arms with a dolphin kick (see p. 103). Try backstroke arms with dolphin kick. Swim double-arm backstroke with a flutter kick or dolphin kick.

Unconventional Kicking Series. Kick in the following manner:
- Flutter kick on the right side 25 yards, then on the left side the next 25 yards. Continue alternating sides.
- Kick dolphin kick on the right side 25 yards, and then on the left side 25 yards. Alternate every length.
- Kick breaststroke on your back.
- Kick breaststroke kick with hands on your buttocks, palms up.
- Vertical dolphin kick. In a vertical position in the water, dolphin kick for a period of time. Then lift your hands out of the water and continue dolphin kicking. Lastly lift your arms out of the water and kick dolphin kick. You will find you will have to work progressively harder as you lift your arms out of the water.
- Kick flutter kick without a kickboard, keeping your face out of the water.
- Eggbeater kick with your hands out of the water. At the sound of a whistle, move to your right a specified distance; at a second whistle, move to your left a specified distance. The instructor blowing the whistle can then change the directions at varying intervals by blowing the whistle and pointing in the direction he or she desires the group to move. In water polo, this drill is called "walking."

Unconventional Breaststroke Pulling. Sit on a kickboard as if riding it like a horse. Pull breaststroke 25 yards in this position, then pull 50 yards in regular breaststroke position. Continue alternating throughout the series. You may wish to use the pull-buoy on the regular breaststroke pull if you have trouble maintaining body position.

In and Out Swim. Swim 25 yards any stroke, get out of the pool, do 5 pushups, and dive back in, swimming another stroke the second 25 yards. Repeat as many times as desired.

Water Pushups. Place hands on deck, push body up and out of the water waist high. Start with 5 repetitions, and work up to 20 repetitions.

Pair Swimming. Your partner pulls while you hold onto his or her legs and kick. Use with front crawl stroke.

50-Yard Individual Medley. Swim butterfly first half of the first 25, backstroke the second half of the first 25, breaststroke the first half of the second 25, and front crawl the second half of the second 25.

Follow the Leader. Using eight lanes, start swimming down Lane 1 using head-up front crawl, back Lane 2 kicking head-up flutter, down Lane 3 unconventional breaststroke pull drill, back Lane 4 elementary backstroke. Continue until you get to Lane 8. Swim underwater to starting point, and begin again, doing other skills or strokes.

Finally, remember that music is a motivator in and of itself. During kicking and swimming drills, arrange for music to be played (select your favorite type).

CHAPTER 5

Minor Annoyances: Some Healthy Advice

Swimming is safer than most vigorous activities. Broken bones, head injuries, and muscle tears are practically unheard of. Nevertheless, you may encounter some minor physical and mental annoyances as you train. These include eye irritations, ear infections, and shoulder and knee pains. We would also like to clear up some misconceptions about training in general and about swim training in particular. These include the unfounded beliefs that (1) swimming increases the incidence of colds and respiratory infections, and (2) women should not train during menstruation or pregnancy. We'll begin with what was once the most common complaint among swimmers: eye irritation.

My Eyes Are Killing Me

Before goggles became a common training aid (about 1970), swimmers suffered from painful bloodshot eyes for hours after a workout. Eye irritation is no longer a serious problem because most swimmers wear goggles while training. Nevertheless, occasionally you may forget your goggles, or they may leak, and your eyes become irritated.

The usual reasons for eye irritation are an imbalance in the pH of the water (the balance between acidity and alkalinity) or an excessive amount of chlorine (the disinfectant used to purify the pool water). Generally the chlorine content and the pH of pool water are maintained at nonirritating levels; that is, between .04 and 1.0 parts per million for chlorine, and between 7.2 and 7.6 for the pH. Unfortunately, the chemical balance of pool water can change for the worse rather rapidly when exposed to sunlight, wind, and sudden changes in water or air temperatures.

If your eyes should become irritated, wash them out with tap water. Don't rub them, and don't use an eye wash without first consulting a physician. Some eye washes may contain chemicals that react adversely with the chemicals in the pool water.

We repeat: *wear goggles when you train*. If you do, you will have no problem with eye irritation.

Earaches

The term "swimmer's ear" refers to a rashlike inflammation of the ear canal that is caused by frequent exposure to moisture. Swimmers often don't dry their ears thoroughly after training, and the remaining moisture causes the warm, dark ear canal to become a "natural breeding ground" for fungi and bacteria. Dry your ears thoroughly with a towel after showering to prevent this from occurring.

Many ear specialists also recommend that you put a few drops of some acetic acid (vinegar) solution in your ears after showering. Several commercial products can be used for this purpose; for example, Swim Ear. Do not use alcohol, because it tends to dissolve the fatty acids in the waxy substance that protects the ear canal.

Use an ear dropper to administer the drying agent. Under no circumstances should you insert pointed or even padded objects beyond the outer opening of your ear canal. Don't risk a perforated ear drum.

Those of you who are prone to ear infections might consider purchasing a pair of ear plugs. An ear specialist can fit a pair that will keep water out of your ears during training. We do not recommend ear plugs that are sold over the counter. They usually don't fit well enough to keep water out of the ear canal, and they can irritate the canal.

Sore Shoulders

A certain amount of soreness is normal during the first few weeks of training. This will pass. However, if you experience shoulder pains later, after you have been training for several weeks or months, you may be developing tendinitis. The pain associated with tendinitis is usually caused by friction when the various ligaments and tendons of the shoulder rub against the bony articulations as you stroke through the water. The constant friction may, in time, cause the soft tissues to become inflamed and swollen, which causes a further increase in friction. A vicious cycle thus develops, leading to chronic shoulder pain.

Some swimmers' shoulders are more vulnerable to this condition than others. A predisposition toward tendinitis may be due to the inherited structure of the shoulder. It may also be due to improper stroke mechanics. As we mentioned earlier, the use of hand paddles may also be a predisposing factor.

Tendinitis is not a common occurrence among swimmers. Nevertheless, the incidence is sufficient to include some advice for preventing this condition. The first sign of tendinitis is a shoulder that hurts after practice. Later in the season, the pain may also be present during practice. Don't wait until the condition becomes severe before you seek professional advice. You should see an orthopedic specialist if you experience posttraining shoulder pain for several days in a row. He or she will probably advise you to apply ice to the painful area after each workout.

You can reduce the probability of developing chronic tendinitis by following the doctor's advice and by adjusting your training so that an inflamed tendon or ligament is permitted a chance to recover. This can be done by swimming strokes that do not require out-of-water arm recoveries. The breaststroke, sidestroke, and elementary backstroke are ideal for this purpose.

Knee Pain

Occasionally swimmers experience pain along the inner borders of their knees when they swim the breaststroke and elementary backstroke. This is because the kicks used in these two strokes require an outward rotation of your lower legs during the propulsive phase. Unfortunately, your knee joints are so constructed that they permit only limited outward rotation, and attempts to rotate them in this way can cause friction between the leg bones and the ligaments on the insides of your knees (the medial collateral ligaments). As a result, these ligaments can become stretched, inflamed, and painful. When pain of this type persists over several days, do not swim the breaststroke and elementary backstroke in training until the pain has subsided. In the meantime, you should consult an orthopedic specialist.

"Aachooo"

One of the most persistent and erroneous bits of misinformation about swimming is that swimming increases your susceptibility to colds and respiratory infections. Nothing could be further from the truth. Colds and respiratory infections are caused by viruses that are transmitted from person to person. The fact that you are cold and wet does not increase your susceptibility to these viruses. You are more likely to catch a cold in a warm, dry, crowded room than in a swimming pool. In fact, research shows that schoolchildren who swim during the winter months miss less school due to colds and respiratory infections than their nonswimming counterparts.

Should you swim when you have a cold? Many people do. Use your own judgment in this matter. There is no need to train when you are ill and unable to enjoy the workout. You can always make up for lost time later. On the other hand, those of you who hate to miss a workout should know that minor colds need not be a deterrent. Swimming will not make your cold worse, nor will it delay your recovery.

But a *severe* cold or respiratory infection presents an entirely different situation. Your resistance to other, more serious infections, will be low when you suffer from a serious respiratory infection. In this case the stress of hard training may lower your resistance even more and could lead to more serious complications. When you have a severe cold or respiratory infection, you should consult a physician and get plenty of rest.

For Women Only

Many women continue to believe that it is unwise, even dangerous, to train when they are menstruating. There is no truth to this belief. Another misconception is that women should not swim during pregnancy. We want to discuss these two misconceptions in the following sections.

Menstruation

Most studies have indicated that women can train during menstruation without fear of illness or injury. In fact, women who suffer from dysmenorrhea may reduce their discomfort by exercising.

This advice notwithstanding, we realize that a small number of female readers may experience particularly painful cramps during menstrual flow. If you are in this category, you may want to reduce the distance and intensity of your training, or you may prefer to refrain from training altogether until the cramps subside. Use your judgment in this matter. You need not be concerned that a few missed workouts each month will keep you from reaching your training goals.

Before leaving this topic, we should mention that some of you may experience cyclic irregularity while you are training. It is not unusual for some women to experience an occasional missed period when they are training. There are also some women whose menstrual flow may be either heavier or lighter than usual. Don't be concerned if you experience one of these conditions. These irregularities will disappear when you adjust to your training regimen. Regardless of what we have just said, if the extent of your cyclic irregularities becomes a source of concern, you can take the precaution of consulting a gynecologist.

Pregnancy

Research indicates that women who train during pregnancy spend less time in labor and have easier deliveries. Also, pregnant women who maintain their muscle tone and aerobic fitness will regain their figures more rapidly after delivery. For these and other reasons, many physicians are now recommending that women train during pregnancy.

Swimming is one of the safest forms of training for pregnant women. The buoyancy of the water tends to eliminate the potentially dangerous "jarring" that can occur in land activities where the joints must support body weight. In addition, the feeling of weightlessness relieves the lower back pains that many pregnant women experience.

However, women who trained regularly before becoming pregnant cannot continue training *at their previous level.* You should ask your physician for advice on this matter. You should expect to work for less time and at a lower level of intensity. You should also increase your departure times and add more long, slow swims to your training program. You should not swim to the point where you feel uncomfortable.

Also, you will find it more comfortable to train if you make a few adjustments in your stroke mechanics. You should not kick very hard when you swim. This change will reduce the pressure on your back and abdomen and will also allow you to swim longer without becoming fatigued. You will probably find that the breaststroke, sidestroke, and front crawl stroke are the most comfortable strokes to swim late in pregnancy.

During each trimester of your pregnancy, you will feel different. You will note very little difference in your girth measurements during your first trimester; therefore, there will be very little change in how you feel in the water. During this first trimester you will probably feel more tired than usual, but swimming should give you a "pickup." Do not overdo.

During the second trimester, you notice girth changes in the abdomen, hip, and the breast area. Now you will feel a little more buoyant. You will find yourself surfacing faster on the pushoffs from the walls, and your legs will be more buoyant on the back crawl and the elementary backstroke. Sometimes your legs may break the surface of the water. You can avoid this in most instances by changing your head position so that you are looking toward your feet, which drops the lower body in the water.

The third trimester is more uncomfortable standing, sitting, and walking, but not swimming. Now is the best time to be in the water because of the buoyancy that reduces the low back aches and pains. During this period, you may become short of breath during your workout. It is best to swim slower and rest more often to prevent undue stress. This is a time for relaxing in the water as well as maintaining strength and endurance.

Swimming laps is not the only thing you can do during your pregnancy. On the days you don't feel like swimming laps, exercise in the water. You can adapt almost any exercise on land to the water. Here are a few exercises you might like to try.

1. Hold onto the side of the pool or gutter with your back to the pool side. Extend your legs and bring them toward your chest. Move your legs in and out.
2. In the same position as Number 1, pull your knees up and toward one shoulder, creating a twisting action. Extend your legs and repeat to the other side.
3. Stand on the bottom of the pool, facing the wall and holding onto the wall. Lift your right leg straight to the side and up to waist height. Lower the leg to starting position, and repeat 5–10 times on the same side. Change sides. You can also stand with your side to the pool wall and lift your leg to the side.
4. Walk across the pool with hands interlaced behind the head. Start in the shallow water and gradually work up to chest-deep water. Remember: the deeper the water, the more resistance and the more energy required.
5. Try jogging in the water backward, sideward, and forward.
6. Bob rhythmically in the water; make sure you move slowly and relaxed.
7. Hold onto the side of the pool and scissor kick, alternating top leg forward and bottom leg back, top leg back, bottom leg forward.
8. In shoulder-deep water, extend your arms horizontally and circle them backward, then forward.
9. Stand in shoulder-deep water, arms at your sides, palms of your hands facing forward. Lift your hands and arms toward the surface of the water. Turn your hands to a pronated (palms down) position and push down to your sides.
10. Gently bounce forward across the pool as if you were jumping across the pool.

Pregnancy is a natural function of the female body. However, there are a few safety rules that you should pay attention to all the time but especially during pregnancy:

1. At all times, walk slowly on wet surfaces.
2. Swim in water that is approximately 80° F to 86° F (26.7 to 30° C) if you are lap swimming. Don't get chilled. And most physicians do not want you in a Jacuzzi with a temperature over 100° F (37.8° C).
3. Do not overdo. Listen to your body, but don't give up your swimming program entirely. Rest more frequently during your workout.

If you follow your physician's advice, you should not have any problems when you train during pregnancy. Nevertheless, you should take the precaution of informing the lifeguard or swimming instructor that you are pregnant. You should also supply him or her with the name of your physician in the event of some unexpected complication.

Although good stroke mechanics are not a prerequisite for training, workouts are more stimulating and enjoyable if you can swim a variety of strokes reasonably well. The American Red Cross has identified ten different swimming strokes. Of these, the three that you will probably use most frequently in your training are the back crawl stroke, the breaststroke, and the front crawl stroke or freestyle.* These three strokes are used in competitive swim meets. There is also a fourth competitive stroke, the butterfly. Some people think the butterfly is too difficult for the noncompetitor to master. That is not so. If you can't swim the butterfly, you should make an effort to learn how. It is enjoyable to swim, once learned, and is a stimulating stroke to use in training. The mechanics of these four competitive strokes are described in Chapter 8.

Of the six remaining noncompetitive strokes, four are resting strokes. That is, they incorporate a glide phase at the end of each stroke cycle. This glide reduces the energy cost of swimming those strokes and makes them

*According to the rules of competitive swimming, an athlete may swim any stroke in a freestyle event. However, since swimmers invariably select the fastest stroke, they swim the front crawl in these races. Therefore, the terms *freestyle* and *front crawl stroke* have become synonymous.

less suitable for training. This fact notwithstanding, some of you may enjoy swimming the sidestroke, the overarm sidestroke, and the elementary backstroke in training. Therefore, the mechanics of these three strokes are described in Chapter 8.

The three strokes that are left — the trudgeon stroke, the trudgeon crawl, and the inverted backstroke — are inferior versions of other strokes. They are seldom swum in training or otherwise, and will not be described.

The descriptions of each stroke are accompanied by photographs that show the correct body positions, the major propulsive phases of the armstrokes and kicks, the recovery motions, and the correct timing between the armstrokes and kicks. After the stroke descriptions, we discuss common problems you may encounter when attempting to improve your stroke mechanics.

The techniques that we recommend may differ from those you were taught by a relative, friend, or previous swimming teacher. Therefore, we would like to acquaint you with some fundamental principles of hydrodynamics before describing the strokes. They will help you understand the physical bases for the techniques we recommend.

The Importance of Swimming Efficiently

You may have been told there is a difference between the stroke mechanics of competitive swimmers and noncompetitive swimmers. Don't believe it. You must adhere to the same fundamental principles of hydrodynamics whether you are interested in swimming faster or in swimming more efficiently.

Swimming efficiently is a matter of using the least amount of energy to propel your body forward at the desired speed. To do so you must not only apply propulsive force in the most economic manner, but you must also reduce the resistance that the water exerts against your body as you move forward. This resistance to forward motion is called *drag,* a term you'll be reading frequently in this chapter. In the next two sections, we discuss ways of applying propulsive force and reducing drag.

Applying Propulsive Force

A recent reexamination of the principles of hydrodynamic propulsion has resulted in some major adjustments of swimming mechanics, particularly as they concern the propulsive potential of the vertical and lateral motions of swimmers' limbs. At one time it was believed that all swimming propulsion was a result of pushing your limbs directly backward through the water. The basis for this theory was Newton's Third Law of Motion: "For every action there is an equal and opposite reaction." Pushing the limbs backward was believed to create a reaction that would propel swimmers forward. Any deviation of the limbs from their backward direction was believed to be wasted motion.

We now realize that swimmers use their limbs more like propellers than like paddles. They push water backward, but they do so with complex three-dimensional sweeping motions that include a predominance of lateral and vertical limb motions and a minimum of backward motion. The stroke patterns for the four competitive strokes in Figure 6.1 show this relationship clearly. The patterns trace the path of swimmers' index fingers through the water. Notice the predominance of up, down, in, and out hand movements in these strokes. Notice also that their hands move backward for only a short distance in each stroke.

The original concept of pushing water backward was correct. However, the application of this concept was obviously in error. Newton's Third Law of Motion remains the primary physical law involved in swimming, yet it is evident that swimmers need not push their limbs backward to push water backward. They apparently use their arms and legs like propeller blades, pushing water backward while they sweep them in predominantly lateral and vertical directions.

The explanation that has been offered for the preponderance of vertical and lateral limb motions in the stroke patterns of highly skilled swimmers is that those swimmers are using *lift* forces for propulsion. Lift forces are common in both aerodynamic and hydrodynamic propulsion. The wings of airplanes and the propellers (which are really rotating wings) and the outboard motors of boats create lift forces that propel those vehicles. It appears that swimmers use their limbs like propeller blades to deflect water backward while sweeping their arms and legs upward, downward, inward, and outward. The widespread belief that they are using their hands like paddles probably results from the fact that the pressure of the water that is being deflected backward gives them the false impression that they are pushing their limbs backward against the water.

How do lift forces work? Let's use the example of the freestyle (front crawl) swimmer in Figure 6.2 to illustrate this phenomenon. He is pressing downward and slightly outward (although this component of motion cannot be seen from a side view) in the first part of his underwater armstroke. Notice that his hand and forearm are pitched in such a way that they deflect the water backward from fingertips to elbow. This backward deflection of the water, in accordance with Newton's Third Law of Motion, creates an

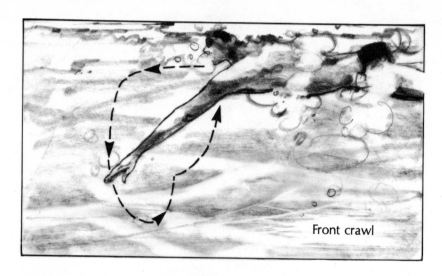

Front crawl

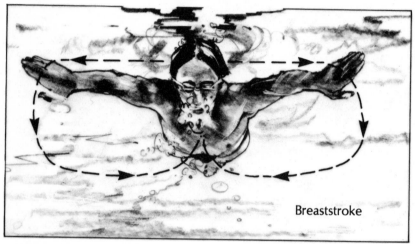

Breaststroke

Figure 6.1. Stroke patterns for the four competitive strokes

equal and opposite counterforce that propels the swimmer forward. The name that has been given to that counterforce is *lift*.

It is unfortunate that the term *lift* is used to describe this propelling force. It invites visions of objects moving upward, when, in actuality, lift force can be exerted in any direction that is perpendicular to the direction that the limbs are moving through the water. In swimming, the lift force is usually exerted in a forward or nearly forward direction.

Space does not permit us to illustrate how swimmers use lift for propul-

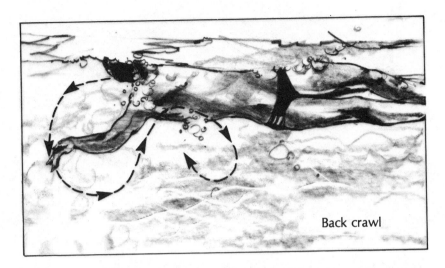

Back crawl

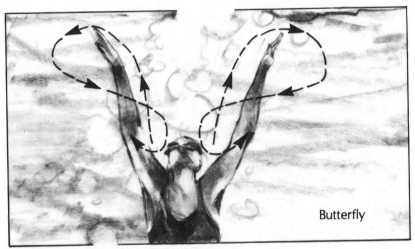

Butterfly

Figure 6.1. (continued)

sion in other strokes, but this example does show how the lateral and vertical limb motions of swimmers can be propulsive.

Proper Hand and Foot Pitch Are Also Important

We will make repeated references to the pitch of the hands and feet as we describe the strokes in the following chapters. You'll notice that the

Figure 6.2. Use of lift force for propulsion in front crawl stroke

swimmers in the photographs in the next chapters seldom have their hands or feet facing directly backward. They pitch them at slight angles to the backward direction so that the water will be deflected backward as it passes over their hands and feet from their leading to trailing edges. When we discuss the various strokes, we include descriptions of the proper hand and foot pitch.

There are two possible explanations why highly skilled swimmers prefer three-dimensional propeller-like movements over two-dimensional paddle-like backward pushes:

1. The propeller-like limb motions extend the distance over which propulsive force can be applied. Using the analogy that a straight line is the closest distance between two points, a straight backward push shortens the propulsive phase of the underwater armstroke, requiring more strokes per length and a greater energy expenditure.
2. Attempting to push water directly backward also requires very rapid strokes with an accompanying increase in energy expenditure. Once water starts to move backward, it gains momentum, and the only way that you can continue to apply propulsive force is to accelerate the backward speed of your limbs beyond the backward speed of the water. On the other hand, circular, three-dimensional stroke patterns allow swimmers to accelerate water backward for a short distance and then to change directions and search for another "handful of quiet water" to accelerate backward.

The purpose of the previous discussion of hydrodynamic principles was to convince those of you who may have been indoctrinated with the "push backward to go forward" theory of drag propulsion that lateral and vertical limb motions play an important role in human swimming propulsion. They are not superfluous, "feathering," movements nor examples of faulty mechanics. They contribute greatly to efficient propulsion. Therefore, you should be sure to use them when you swim the various strokes.

Reducing Drag

The illustrations in Figure 6.3 show that drag is increased when swimmers' positions are less than horizontal with the water's surface. Drag is also increased when their bodies are not aligned laterally; that is, when they wiggle from side to side as they swim down the pool. A certain amount of sideward rotation and upward and downward body motion is needed to apply propulsive force effectively. However, when these motions are excessive (see Figures 6.3 and 6.5), they cause a dramatic increase in water turbulence, which in turn increases drag.

Swimming with one's face out of the water is the most common cause of poor horizontal alignment. Most inexperienced swimmers do so in the mistaken notion that it is easier to "catch a breath" in this position. Unfortunately, their hips and feet drop deeper in the water to compensate for the weight they are supporting above the surface, and the drag on their bodies is increased. In Figure 6.3, the swimmer's body is inclined downward exces-

Figure 6.3. Effect of poor horizontal alignment on drag

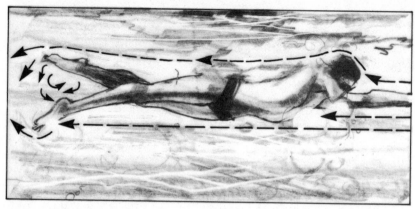

Figure 6.4. Side view of front crawl stroke, showing excellent horizontal alignment

sively from head to feet; this increases the amount of water his body encounters and the amount of effort he must exert to propel himself forward.

You can reduce drag by lowering your head and assuming a streamlined position in the water so that your entire body is nearly horizontal with the surface. A streamlined freestyle (front crawl) swimmer (see Figure 6.4) takes up very little space in the water and therefore encounters less drag.

Unfortunately, it is not always possible to maintain a horizontal body position. The mechanics of some strokes — principally the breaststroke, butterfly, and sidestroke — require that you deviate from a horizontal position somewhat in order to apply propulsive force more effectively. In these cases a tradeoff is required. You must allow some slight increase of drag in order to apply a large amount of propulsive force. Nevertheless, in order to apply propulsive force effectively, you should seek a body position that will result in the least possible increase of drag when you must be less than horizontal with the surface.

The most common cause of poor lateral alignment is recovering the arms over the water in a wide, roundhouse manner (see Figure 6.5). The forceful outward motion of the swimmer's arm tends to pull the hips outward in the same direction. Since the body is unsupported in the water, the outward force of the hip exerts a counterforce on the legs that swings them outward in the opposite direction. As you would expect, these excessive sideward movements increase drag rather dramatically. Poor lateral alignment is only a problem in the front and back crawl strokes, where the arms are recovered over the water in an alternate manner. In strokes where the arms are recovered simultaneously, any potentially disruptive movements of one limb are offset by movements of the other limb that are in equal and opposite directions.

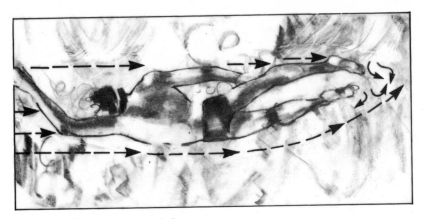

Figure 6.5. Effect of poor lateral alignment on drag

One of the most important skills for maintaining good lateral alignment you must learn is to roll your body. Good swimmers roll their entire bodies from side to side in the front and back crawl strokes. This allows them to stroke more efficiently, and — equally important — it tends to reduce unwanted sideward body movements. The photographs of front and back crawl swimmers in Chapter 7 show these rolling motions clearly. You will probably be surprised by the amount of body roll that they display. They roll their bodies downward from the surface approximately 45 degrees to each side. Take our word for it, this is not an excessive amount of body roll. Most good swimmers use this amount in these strokes. If you were taught to swim in a flat position, retrain yourself. You'll find that rolling your body from side to side will improve your efficiency immensely when you swim the front and back crawl strokes.

CHAPTER 7

The Competitive Strokes

In this chapter, we describe the mechanics of the four competitive strokes: the front crawl or freestyle, the back crawl or backstroke, the breaststroke, and the butterfly. We also describe the turns that are used with these strokes.

The Front Crawl Stroke, or Freestyle

The front crawl is the fastest and most efficient swimming stroke. You will probably swim it more frequently than any other stroke in your training sessions.

For explanation purposes, we have divided the mechanics of the front crawl stroke into the following sections: the body position, the arm recovery and breathing, the underwater armstroke, the kick, and the timing of the arms and legs. We also describe the flip turn that is used by front crawl swimmers in competition and training.

Body Position

The photograph in Figure 7.1, taken from a side view, shows the correct body position for front crawl swimming. The swimmer's body is hori-

70

Figure 7.1. Side view of front crawl stroke, showing excellent body position

zontal with the surface. Her head is underwater; the waterline is at her hairline. Her feet remain within the confines of her trunk during most of the kick. She does not kick downward excessively, because doing so would increase drag more than it would increase propulsive force.

As noted earlier, poor horizontal alignment usually results from carrying one's head too high out of the water. Be sure to put your face in the water so that the waterline is somewhere between your hairline and the middle of your head. Focus your eyes forward and downward.

Arm Recovery and Breathing

The sequence of photographs in Figure 7.2 shows a swimmer using a high-elbow recovery and a traditional breathing style.

Breathing. She is rotating her face toward the right for a breath in Photos A and B. She does this during the final half of her right underwater armstroke. At the same time, her left arm has entered the water and is stretching downward, allowing her to rotate her body smoothly toward the right so that she can breathe without lifting her face out of the water. She inhales during the first half of the right arm recovery (see Photo C), and she returns her face to the water during the second half (see Photos D to F).

Efficient swimmers do not hold their breath at any time when they swim the front crawl, or, for that matter, when they swim any stroke. They exhale very slowly and steadily, timing the exhalation so that they will not need another breath until they are, once again, in the position shown in Photos B and C of Figure 7.2. If you exhale too quickly, the almost immediate need for air will cause you to rush through your armstrokes to get into position for another breath.

The direction you turn your head is a matter of personal preference. Most swimmers turn their faces to the right. However, if you are comfortable breathing to the left, use that side.

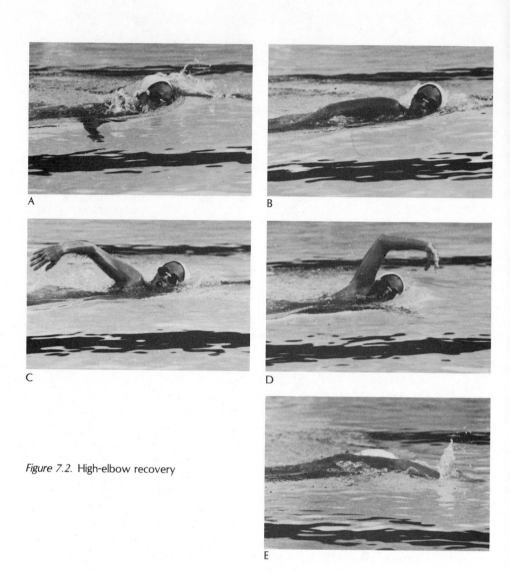

Figure 7.2. High-elbow recovery

Arm Recovery. The recovery should be a relaxed swing of your arm over the water. This is the time when you rest your muscles in preparation for another underwater stroke. The recovery begins with the release of pressure on the water as your hand passes your thigh at the end of the underwater armstroke. Your arm is now traveling upward and outward. Therefore, you can simply relax and let the momentum of your arm carry it out of the water and through the first portion of the recovery.

Your elbow leaves the water first (see Photo B of Figure 7.2), followed by your hand (see Photo C). Carry your arm over the water with your elbow flexed and your hand close to your body. It is important to roll your body toward the recovering arm in order to facilitate this recovery motion.

When your hand passes your head, begin reaching forward for the entry (see Photo D). Make the entry directly in front of your shoulder, with your arm slightly flexed at the elbow. In this way, your hand will enter the water first with your elbow and then your shoulder entering in very nearly the same spot (see Photo E).

You hand should enter the water on its side, with your palm facing diagonally outward. Then extend that arm forward while you finish the underwater stroke with your other arm.

The recovery of the other arm is executed in a similar manner (see Photos F to I). Although you will not breathe on that side, you should roll your body in that direction to facilitate the high-elbow action and prevent disruption of lateral alignment.

Alternate Breathing

Some swimmers prefer to take their breaths using a style known as *alternate* or *bilateral breathing*. Swimmers who use this method breathe

Figure 7.2. (continued)

F

G

H

I

A

B

C

D

E

F

Figure 7.3. Front underwater view of front crawl stroke

both to their right and to their left. They take two breaths during every three arm cycles (rather than one breath per arm cycle, as we have recommended).

Swimmers who use this procedure breathe to the right side as shown by the swimmer in Figure 7.2. They leave their faces in the water during the next two armstrokes and then breathe to the left side as they complete their left armstroke. Following this, they take two more strokes without breathing and then breathe to their right, once again. It's not as complicated as it sounds. Try it in front of a mirror a few times, and you'll see how easy it is to learn alternate breathing.

Proponents of alternate breathing believe this method encourages swimmers to roll their bodies to both sides, with the result that their right and left armstrokes are equally propulsive. (Many swimmers stroke less efficiently with the arm opposite their breathing side because they do not roll their bodies far enough in that direction.) They reason that it is a good tradeoff to give up one breath every three armstrokes for more propulsive force. Those who oppose this method feel that the additional breath is more important than the small increase in stroking efficiency that might occur. Try both methods and decide for yourself.

Underwater Armstroke

The swimmer in the series of photographs in Figure 7.3 is shown executing one complete stroke cycle from an underwater front view. The underwater armstroke is composed of five parts: (1) entry and stretch, (2) downsweep, (3) insweep, (4) upsweep, and (5) release.

Figure 7.3. (continued)

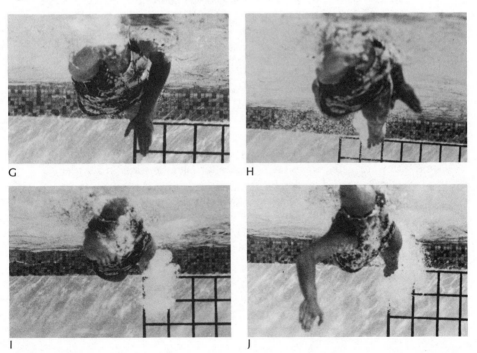

G H

I J

Entry and Stretch (Photo A). The swimmer's left arm enters the water when she is midway through her right underwater armstroke. She stretches it forward while she completes the propulsive phase of her right armstroke.

Downsweep (Photos B and C). When her right arm releases the water in Photo B, she begins the propulsive phase of her left armstroke by pressing downward and slightly outward. She continues to press downward and outward until her hand is nearly two feet underwater and her entire arm is facing backward (see Photo C). The palm of her hand should be facing backward, and slightly outward during this portion of the armstroke.

The downsweep is a gentle, stretching movement where you feel the water pressure. Do not try to apply propulsive force until you have the water behind your arm, or you will push your body upward and thus will slow down.

Insweep (Photos D to F). In Photo C, she made a "catch"; that is, she began to apply force to the water. Now she sweeps her hand backward, inward, and upward under her chest. She gradually bends her arm during the insweep until it is flexed approximately 90 degrees at the elbow, when her hand is under her chest. She slowly rotates her palm inward, upward, and backward as it travels under her body.

Upsweep (Photos G and H). As she nears completion of the insweep, she makes an abrupt change of direction and sweeps her hand backward, outward, and upward toward the surface. Her palm is rotated to an outward- and backward-facing position during this final portion of the underwater armstroke.

Release (Photo I). She releases the water as her left hand passes her thigh. At this point, she turns her palm inward so that her hand can slip upward out of the water and into the recovery with the least resistance.

Her right arm enters the water and stretches forward as she completes the second half of her left underwater armstroke. Once her left arm releases the water, she strokes her right arm through the water in a similar pattern (see Photos I, J, A, and B).

Please notice that she rolls her body approximately 45 degrees to each side as she sweeps her arms through the water. The extent of her body roll is particularly evident in Photos C and I, although she is rolled to one side or the other during almost the entirety of the stroke cycle.

The Flutter Kick

The flutter kick is illustrated in the series of photographs in Figure 7.4. It consists of an upbeat and downbeat. We'll describe the action of one leg, beginning with the downbeat.

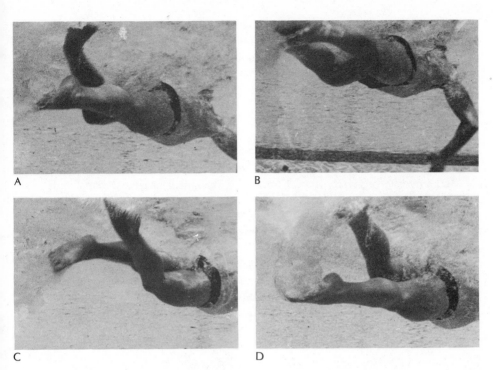

A   B

C   D

Figure 7.4. Flutter kick used in front crawl stroke

Downbeat of Left Leg (Photos A to D). The downbeat begins as the swimmer's left leg passes his right on its way upward. He begins the downbeat by flexing at the hip and pushing his thigh downward. His lower leg and ankle are relaxed so that the pressure of the water beneath pushes them upward until his knee is flexed and his toes are pointed upward and backward (see Photo C). At that point he kicks his lower leg downward by extending it at the knee. Notice that the roll of his body also causes him to kick outward. The downbeat is completed when his leg is completely straight and just below his body (see Photo D).

A good toe point is essential to an effective flutter kick. Be sure your toes are facing up and in during the downbeat (see left foot in Photo B and right foot in Photo C).

Upbeat of Right Leg (Photos A to D). The upbeat is a reboundlike action in which the swimmer's thigh begins moving upward as his lower leg is completing the downbeat. Once his leg is extended, he sweeps it up until it passes above his other leg. The next downbeat begins at that point.

The pressure of the water above his leg will maintain it in an extended position during the upbeat. One of the most common mistakes that novice swimmers make is to bend their knees during the upbeat. This retards their forward speed because their lower legs push forward as well as upward against the water. Be sure to sweep your legs up from the hip with a relaxed lower leg and ankle.

Timing of Arms and Legs

The most effective timing of the arms and legs has been a matter of controversy for several years. Competitive swimmers have set national and world records using a variety of rhythms; so it has been impossible to determine which method is best. The most enduring rhythms have been the two-beat kick, the two-beat crossover kick, the four-beat kick, and the six-beat kick.

How can you determine which of these rhythms is right for you? With training, most swimmers "fall into" the pattern that is best for them. After a few weeks or months of training, you'll probably notice that your legs are kicking in a regular pattern with your armstroke. Don't be concerned if this sequence has some irregularities such as missed beats, sideward kicks, or legs that cross over one another. These "irregularities" are quite common.

Two-Beat Kick. In the two-beat kick, there are two leg kicks to each arm cycle, timed as follows. The left leg is kicked down as the left arm completes its underwater stroke. The rhythm is similar on the other side, with the right leg kicking down when that arm completes its underwater stroke. The legs hesitate or "drag" between kicks.

The two-beat kick requires less leg muscle activity than any other rhythm. Therefore, it has become a favorite of many distance swimmers and triathletes, who use it to save energy. It is particularly popular with female swimmers. Many male swimmers (and some female swimmers) seem to need more beats to keep their bodies aligned and near the surface. Some of these swimmers use the next rhythm that we're going to describe, the two-beat crossover kick.

Two-Beat Crossover Kick. The two-beat crossover kick is really a four-beat rhythm with two major and two minor leg beats per stroke cycle. The two major beats follow exactly the same pattern as described for the two-beat kick. However, instead of "dragging" the legs between beats, a swimmer who uses this method crosses one leg over the other. The left leg crosses over the right in a minor beat just after the swimmer completes the downbeat of the right leg. In turn, the right leg crosses over the left after the left leg has completed its downbeat. It seems to be a compromise rhythm that allows swimmers to conserve some energy while also maintaining good alignment.

Six-Beat Kick. The six-beat kick is the most common rhythm used by swimmers. It is also the most precise and logical rhythm. There are six leg kicks to each stroke cycle, or three kicks per armstroke. Each kick accompanies one of the arm sweeps described previously. We describe the timing for the left armstroke (the pattern is identical for the right).

The first of three kicks occurs with your left leg as your left arm sweeps downward at the beginning of the underwater armstroke. Kick downward with your right leg as your left arm sweeps in and up under your body. Kick down with your left leg, once again, as your left arm sweeps out and up toward the surface.

On the right side, kick your right leg down during the downsweep and upsweep. Kick your left leg down during the insweep.

Four-Beat Kick. The four-beat kick is a combination of the two- and six-beat rhythms just described. A two-beat timing is used with one armstroke and a six-beat timing with the other. The sequence is described with the two-beat timing coupled with the right armstroke and the six-beat timing with the left. Of course, the sequence would be reversed if the two-beat timing occurred during the left armstroke.

Kick your right leg down as your right arm completes the upsweep and insweep of its underwater stroke. Then execute three kicks during the left armstroke. These kicks follow the same pattern described for the six-beat kick. That is, kick down with the left leg during the downsweep and upsweep, and kick down with the right leg during the insweep.

Don't Kick Too Hard

Regardless of the rhythm you use, do not kick hard or powerfully when you swim the front crawl. Most experienced swimmers (sprinters excepted) use their kick like a rudder, to stabilize the body, and they derive most of the propulsion from the armstroke. This is because the vigorous use of the large muscles of your legs more than doubles the energy cost of swimming while adding only slightly to your speed. You'll swim at an average faster speed for longer distances if you reduce the effort you expend in kicking to the minimum that is needed to maintain your body in proper alignment. A good drill for determining this minimum kick that you should use is described in Chapter 9.

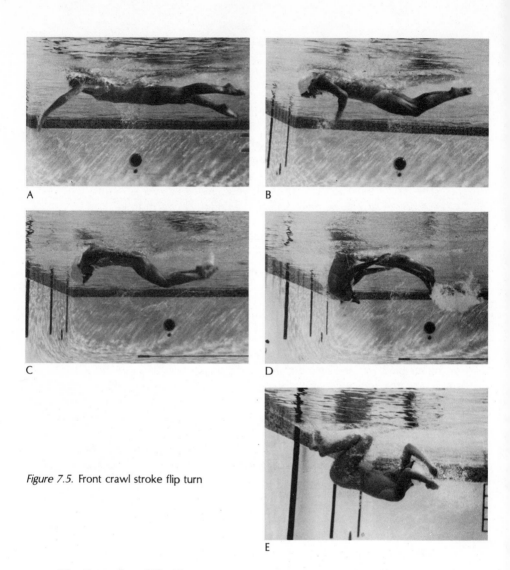

Figure 7.5. Front crawl stroke flip turn

The Front Crawl Flip Turn

The flip (somersault) turn is the fastest way to change directions when you reach the end of the pool. The photographs in Figure 7.5 show a swimmer executing this turn. You do not need to use the flip turn in training. Nevertheless, it is a fast and skilled method of turning, and you may want to learn it.

With one stroke to go before she reaches the wall, the swimmer in Figure 7.5 leaves her right arm at her side, rather than recovering it over the water (see Photo A). She sweeps her left hand back so that both hands are at her hips, and she begins to somersault forward into the wall. She initiates the somersault by ducking her head and executing a small dolphin kick that pushes her hips upward and forward into the somersault (see Photos B and C).

She drives her head downward and then upward as she tucks her legs and somersaults into the wall (see Photos D and E). Notice that she turns her palms down and pushes downward on the water to help pull her head toward the surface during the last half of the somersault.

She has completed the somersault in Photo F, and she plants her feet on the wall to prepare for the pushoff. She is on her back, and she is approximately two feet underwater when she plants her feet. Her toes are pointed sideward and upward. Her hands are overhead, and her trunk is aligned with her feet so that she can push off without delay.

She drives off the wall by extending both her arms and legs, and she rotates toward a face down (prone) position during the pushoff and glide that follow (see Photos G and H). She glides in a streamlined position until she begins to lose speed. Then she executes two or three kicks and one armstroke that bring her body to the surface where she can resume swimming the front crawl (see Photo I).

Figure 7.5. (continued)

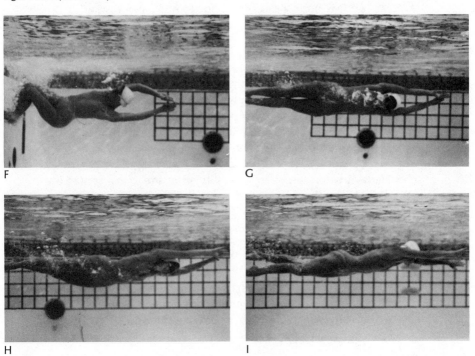

F   G

H   I

Be sure to streamline your body during the pushoff. This gives you maximum speed and distance "off the wall." Your body should be in perfect alignment from fingertips to toes. Your arms should be stretched tightly overhead. Your head should be between your arms, and your legs should be completely extended.

Some Common Problems

PROBLEM: "I swallow water when I take a breath."

SOLUTION: You are probably exhaling after your mouth comes out of the water. This delays your inhalation until your face is returning into the water, so you inhale a mixture of water and air. Be sure to blow all your air out as you turn your face toward the surface. By doing so, you will be ready to inhale when your mouth reaches the surface.

PROBLEM: "My hips and legs sink when I swim."

SOLUTION: Your kick is weak, and you may be carrying your head too high out of the water. Stretch your ankles, and add more kicking to your workouts to improve your kick. Kicking with fins may also help. Lower your head so that the water surface breaks somewhere between your hairline and the middle of your head.

PROBLEM: "My body wiggles from side to side when I swim."

SOLUTION: You may be making one or more of the following mistakes:

1. You may be swinging your arms to the side during the recovery. Try to use the high-elbow recovery described in Figure 7.2. A good drill for learning a high-elbow recovery is to drag your fingertips through the water as you recover. Keep your hand close to your body as you do so. Later you can lift your hand just high enough to clear the water while recovering it in the same manner.
2. You may be swinging your hand across your face toward the opposite shoulder as it enters the water. This is called *overreaching*. Be sure that your hand enters the water in front of your shoulder. Then reach forward, not inward, as you extend it beneath the surface.
3. You may have your hand facing inward too much as you sweep it under your body. This pulls your body outward in the opposite direction.

PROBLEM: "I bob up and down when I swim."

SOLUTION: You may be pushing water downward in the first part of your underwater stroke, and/or you may be pushing it upward during the final portion. In both cases, your hand is probably pitched incorrectly. That is, it faces almost directly downward during the first part of the stroke and

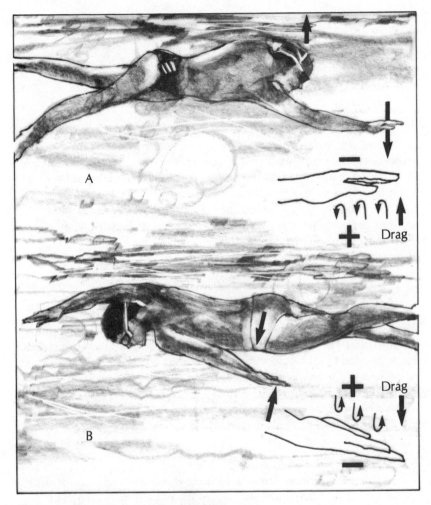

Figure 7.6. Effect of improper hand positions during downward sweep at beginning of underwater armstroke and upward sweep at end of armstroke

upward during the final part. The effect of this error is illustrated in Figure 7.6. The swimmer in Figure 7.6A has not waited until the water is behind his arm before applying propulsive force and pushes downward from the surface, creating a drag force that pushes his body upward. The swimmer in Figure 7.6B has his hand facing upward too much during the final upward sweep of the front crawl stroke. This hand position does not deflect water backward but instead creates a drag force in a downward direction that pulls the swimmer's hips down and decelerates his forward speed. Try pitching your hand so that your palm is facing backward more during these phases of the underwater armstroke.

The Back Crawl Stroke

The back crawl stroke is really very much like the front crawl, with the obvious exception that you are swimming on your back rather than on your stomach. The armstrokes are similar. Both strokes use a flutter kick, and the timing of the arms and legs in the back crawl is identical to the six-beat timing described for the front crawl.

Due to their similarity, we describe the back crawl under the same headings as for the front crawl. Those sections are (1) body position, (2) arm recovery and breathing, (3) underwater armstroke, (4) kick, and (5) timing of arms and legs.

Body Position

The underwater photograph in Figure 7.7, taken from a side view, shows a swimmer with excellent body position. The entire back of his head is in the water. His body is streamlined, with only a slight downward inclination from head to foot. Notice that there is a slight bend at his waist. This minor deviation from the horizontal is necessary to prevent his legs from breaking through the surface when he kicks upward. It is important that he not hold his head out of the water, because doing so would force his hips and legs downward and create additional drag.

Arm Recovery and Breathing

Back crawl swimmers use an alternating armstroke where one arm applies propulsive force underwater while the other is recovered over the water (Figure 7.8).

Figure 7.7. Underwater side view of back crawl stroke, showing correct body position

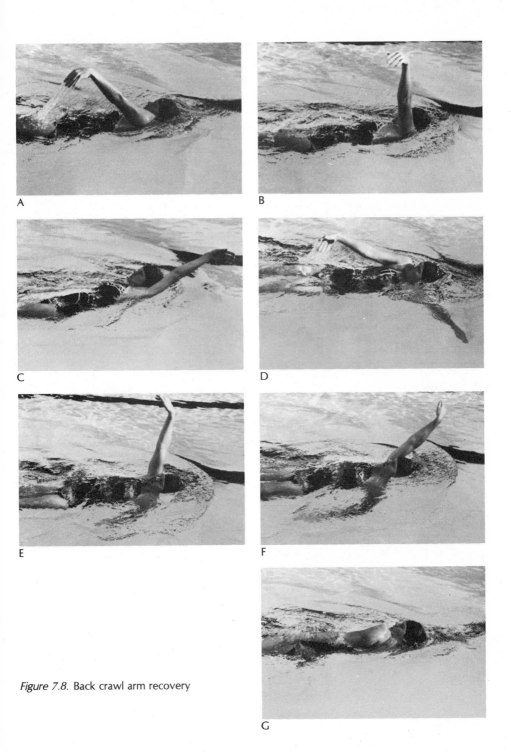

Figure 7.8. Back crawl arm recovery

Arm Recovery. The photographs in Figure 7.8 show a back crawl swimmer recovering her arms over the water. The underwater armstroke should end with the swimmer's hand well below her thigh. She then recovers directly overhead with her arm in a relaxed and completely extended position.

She initiates the recovery of her left arm by rolling her body (but not her head) toward the right side as her right arm enters the water. This rolling action brings her left hand to the surface, after which she swings it straight upward and backward overhead to an entry position directly in front of her left shoulder (see Photos A to D).

As her hand leaves the water, her palm is facing inward (see Photo A). It is rotated outward as it passes overhead (see Photo B). She should enter her hand into the water, on edge, with her palm facing outward (see Photo C). She recovers her left arm in an identical manner (see Photos D to G).

Breathing. One of the major advantages of swimming the back crawl in training is that your face is always above the surface, where you can breathe without concern for swallowing water. You can inhale and exhale at will. However, many swimmers prefer to inhale and exhale once during each stroke cycle (two armstrokes). They inhale during one arm recovery and exhale during the other.

Underwater Armstroke

The underwater armstroke consists of (1) entry, (2) downsweep, (3) upsweep, (4) another downsweep, and (5) release. The sequence of photographs in Figure 7.9, taken from a front underwater view, shows one complete stroke cycle.

Entry (Photo A). The swimmer's left arm is completing its underwater stroke as her right arm enters the water. Her right arm is directly ahead of her shoulder, and her hand is on edge, with palm facing outward.

Downsweep (Photos B and C). After entering the water, she sweeps her left hand down and out until the water is behind her arm. She rotates the palm of her hand from an outward-facing to a downward- and backward-facing position during the downsweep. Notice that the swimmer in these photographs rolls her body considerably to the right to facilitate this downward sweep. As we indicated in Chapter 6, rolling your body at least 45 degrees to each side is important to efficient back crawl swimming.

As was the case in the front crawl stroke, back crawl swimmers should not begin to apply force until their arm is facing backward. Many swimmers make the mistake of trying to push down against the water immediately after their hand enters. This is a mistake because the water is under their arm at this point, and applying force pushes their bodies upward rather than forward.

Upsweep (Photos C and D). Once the water is behind her arm, the swimmer begins sweeping her hand backward, upward, and inward until it is near the surface of the water. She gradually flexes her arm throughout the upsweep until it is bent approximately 90 degrees when her hand nears the surface of the water. The palm of her hand gradually rotates from a downward-facing toward an upward- and backward-facing position during this sweep.

A

Figure 7.9. Underwater armstroke of back crawl

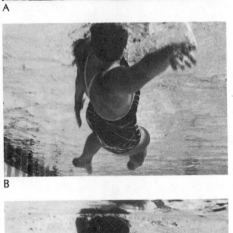

B

C

D

E

(continued)

F

G

H

I

Figure 7.9. (continued)

Second Downsweep (Photos D and E). As her hand nears the top of the upsweep, she begins pushing it backward, downward, and inward until her arm is completely extended and well below her thigh. Her palm is rotated from an upward-facing to a downward-facing position during this time.

Release (Photo F). When the second downsweep has been completed, she releases pressure on the water and turns her palm inward so that her hand can slip upward out of the water with minimal resistance. She allows the roll of her body to carry her hand and arm up and out of the water into the recovery.

Her left arm enters the water as her right arm completes the second downsweep (see Photos E and F). She then sweeps her left arm through the water in the same way (see Photos F to I).

The drawing of a backstroke arm pattern that was presented in Figure 6.1 of Chapter 6 shows an excellent method for visualizing the motions of one underwater armstroke. Think of your hand as tracing a letter "S" that is on its side as you stroke through the water. The first curve of the "S" corresponds to the downsweep. The middle curve is matched with the upsweep, and the final curve is matched to the second downsweep.

Kick

As we mentioned, the flutter kick that is used in the back crawl bears a striking resemblance to the flutter kick of the front crawl. The legs kick up and down in an alternating manner, with the upbeat of one leg beginning simultaneously with the downbeat of the other. The sequence of photographs in Figure 7.10 show the back crawl kick. We describe the action of one leg, starting with the upbeat.

Upbeat of Left Leg (Photos A to C). The upbeat originates from the hip, with the swimmer's thigh being the first part of his leg to move upward. As he kicks up, the pressure of the water above his relaxed lower leg forces it down so that his lower leg is flexed at the knees and his foot is pointed downward and inward (pigeon-toed). He then completes the upbeat by vigorously extending his lower leg upward (see Photos B and C). His leg is completely extended as his foot reaches the surface. Neither his knees nor his foot should break through the surface. However, emphasizing that his big toe may break through the surface of the water is a good teaching technique to ensure a proper upbeat.

Figure 7.10. Flutter kick used in back crawl stroke

A

B

C

D

Notice that the swimmer begins kicking upward and inward in Photo A but finishes the upbeat by kicking up and out (see Photo C). This is so that the kick will coordinate with and assist the natural rolling motions of his body as he strokes through the water. Back crawl swimmers do not kick straight up and down. The execution of the lateral motions improves the effectiveness of this kick.

It is important to allow the water to push your toes downward and inward during the upbeat. This improves the propulsiveness of your kick. If your ankles are not flexible enough to achieve a pigeon-toed position, stretch them with some of the plantarflexing exercises shown in Figure 3.9 of Chapter 3.

Downbeat of Right Leg (Photos A to C). The downbeat of the kick is executed from the hip with a relaxed, straight leg. The pressure of the water beneath the swimmer's descending leg will maintain it in this position. The downbeat continues until his right leg passes below his left (see Photo C). At this point, he lifts his right thigh toward the surface and begins kicking upward.

As in the front crawl stroke, the kick should be easy and rhythmic rather than forceful and heavy. This conserves energy and makes it possible to swim farther and faster with less fatigue.

Timing of Arms and Legs

Nearly all back crawl swimmers use a six-beat kick. This rhythm is pictured in the series of photographs in Figure 7.9. There are three kicks per armstroke, or six kicks per arm cycle. The swimmer's right leg kicks upward as her right arm sweeps down after entering the water (see Photo B). She kicks her left leg upward as her right arm sweeps up and in (see Photo D). Her right leg kicks upward, once again, as she sweeps her right arm down at the end of the underwater armstroke (see Photo F). A similar sequence of arm sweeps and leg kicks occurs during the left armstroke with her left leg kicking up during the downsweep, her right leg kicking up during the insweep, and her left leg kicking up again during the second downsweep. That sequence is shown in Photos G, I, and A.

The Spin Turn

It would take too much space to describe all the turns used in back crawl swimming. Therefore, we describe the turn that seems to be most popular at the present time. It is called a "spin turn," because the swimmers spin around on their backs to change directions (see Figure 7.11).

The first problem you must solve is to find a way of determining when you are approaching the end of the pool for a turn. A set of backstroke

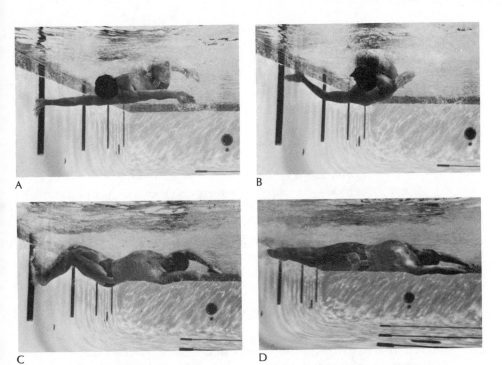

A   B

C   D

Figure 7.11. Back crawl stroke spin turn

flags positioned overhead can help you. They should be positioned exactly 15 feet from each end of the pool. Count the number of strokes you need to swim from the flags to the wall. Once you know this number, you need not waste time and energy looking backward with each stroke as you approach the wall. You can judge when to begin turning by counting strokes each time you pass the flags.

On the last stroke before you reach the wall, extend your arm overhead and downward, placing the palm of your hand on the wall approximately 12–18 inches underwater (see Photo A). Point your fingertips downward. After you touch, lift your legs out of the water and spin them around toward the arm that is in contact with the wall (see Photo B). Keep your head underwater during the spin.

Help the spinning action by pushing your body away from the wall with your contact hand. Meanwhile, use your other arm to help spin by pulling inward toward the top of your head (see Photos A and B).

While you were spinning around, you should have slipped your contact arm forward through the water to meet your other arm overhead, so that you are ready to push off immediately when your feet reach the wall. You should be on your back when your feet make contact, and your hands should be overhead and together, with one hand in the palm of the other (see Photo C).

Push off on your back by extending your arms and legs. Glide through the water in a streamlined position until you begin to lose speed (see Photo D). At that point, you should kick two or three times, pull yourself to the surface with one armstroke, and resume swimming the back crawl stroke.

Some Common Problems

PROBLEM: "My legs sink when I swim."

SOLUTION: You are probably swimming with your head out of the water, and you may have a weak kick. The possible solutions are the same as indicated for a similar problem in the front crawl. Improve your kick with extra kicking drills, use fins to encourage greater ankle flexibility, and lower your head to improve your horizontal body alignment.

PROBLEM: "My body wiggles from side to side when I swim this stroke."

SOLUTION: This problem may have several causes.

1. You may be overreaching. That is, you may be swinging your arm behind your head toward the opposite shoulder as it enters the water. This pushes your hips out of alignment in the opposite direction. Recover your arm straight overhead, and put your hand in the water directly in front of your shoulder. Think of yourself as lying on the face of a clock with your head pointing at 12 o'clock and your feet at 6 o'clock. Your left hand should enter the water at 5 minutes after 12, and your right arm should enter at 5 minutes to 12.

2. You may be pushing your arm outward too forcefully after it enters the water. This pushes your head and shoulders outward in the opposite direction. Sweep your hand down and out gently. Don't attempt to apply propulsive force until your hand is approximately two feet underwater and you can feel the water behind your arm.

3. You may be pushing inward rather than downward during the final half of your underwater armstroke. This pulls your hips and feet outward toward your arm. Extend your arm down and back during the second downsweep, and try to time the extension so that your arm is not completely straight until it is well below your thigh (see Photo F of Figure 7.9).

PROBLEM: "I bob up and down when I swim."

SOLUTION: There are two possible reasons for this problem.

1. You may be pushing down with your arm immediately after it enters the water. The counterforce from this motion pushes your body up.

Don't attempt to apply force until your hand is well underwater and you can feel the water behind, rather than under, your arm.

2. You may have your hand facing upward too much as you sweep it toward the surface during the upsweep. This pulls your body down. Keep your hand facing backward as well as upward as you sweep it toward the surface.

PROBLEM: "My knees break through the surface of the water when I kick."

SOLUTION: You are lifting your thighs up too much during the upbeat of the kick. Put more emphasis on extending your lower leg upward, and do not lift your thigh very much at all.

The Breaststroke

We use a different sequence for describing the mechanics of the breaststroke: (1) armstroke, (2) timing of arms and legs, (3) kick, and (4) body position and breathing.

Armstroke

The breaststroke armstroke is pictured, from a front underwater view, in Figure 7.12. The phases of the armstroke described are (1) outsweep, (2) insweep, and (3) recovery.

Outsweep (Photos A and B). The armstroke begins as the swimmer's legs come together at the end of the kick (see Photo A). At that point, he sweeps his arms directly outward until his hands are outside his shoulders (see Photo B). The palms of his hands should be facing out and back during this sweep. The outward sweep is a gentle motion, with very little force applied until his hands have passed outside his shoulders and the water is behind his arms.

Insweep (Photos B to D). From the end of the outsweep, he presses his hands backward, downward, inward, and upward in a wide, powerful, circular sweep that ends when they come together under his chin. He accomplishes this propeller-like sweep by gradually flexing his elbows as he applies force. He rotates slowly the palms of his hands from an outward-facing to an inward- and upward-facing position during this sweep.

Recovery (Photos D and E). The propulsive phase of the armstroke is completed when his hands come together under his chin. He executes the arm recovery by reaching forward until his arms are completely extended

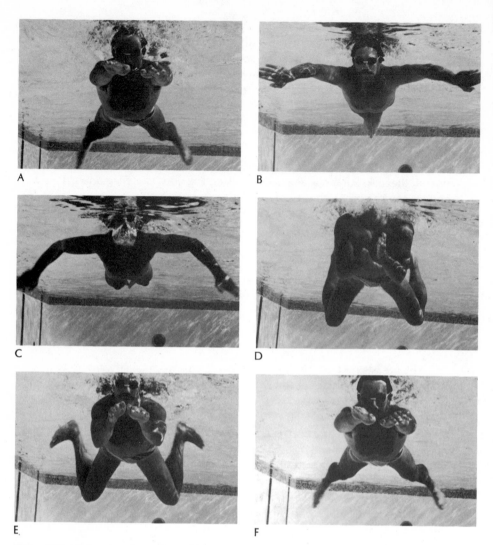

Figure 7.12. Underwater front view of breast-stroke armstroke

in front of his body. His palms are rotated down as he extends his arms forward.

Timing of Arms and Legs

Breaststroke swimmers use an alternate timing where they pull, then kick with very little overlap between these two propulsive phases of the stroke. The swimmer in Figure 7.12 demonstrates this timing very well.

His legs are held together in an extended position in line with his body during the propulsive phase of the armstroke (see Photos B and C). Thus, his body is streamlined, so he is stroking against less resistance.

He begins to recover his legs when his hands sweep upward under his chin. The leg recovery should be completed as he reaches forward, and he executes the thrust phase of his kick as he completes the arm recovery (see Photos D to F).

Kick

The breaststroke incorporates a kick that is quite different from the previous two strokes. Here, swimmers must dorsiflex (flatten) rather than plantarflex (point) their feet. Swimmers who dorsiflex their feet well tend to use this stroke considerably in training. Others may find the kick difficult to master. If you are in the latter group, use some of the dorsiflexing stretching exercises shown in Figure 3.9 of Chapter 3 and make a concerted effort to learn the breaststroke kick. Once you learn it, you will enjoy training with this stroke.

The photographs in Figure 7.13, taken from a diagonal rear view, show clearly the mechanics of an excellent breaststroke kick. This kick will be described in the two parts: the recovery and the thrust.

Recovery (Photos A and B). The swimmer recovers her legs in preparation for the propulsive phase of the kick by flexing at the knees and slipping her legs forward. She reduces drag by keeping her toes pointed backward and by flexing minimally at the hip joints.

Thrust (Photos B to G). As her feet near her buttocks, she begins to circle them outward in preparation for the propulsive phase of the kick. Notice the position of her feet and legs in Photo B. Her feet are flat and facing upward. Her legs are flexed at the hip, with her knees approximately as far apart as her shoulders. You probably can execute an effective kick if you can get your feet and legs in this position as you start the propulsive phase.

She accomplishes the propulsive phase of the kick by sweeping her feet in a circle that is outward, backward, downward, and finally inward. She extends her legs as she executes this sweep. The kick ends with her legs completely extended and the soles of her feet touching together. She slowly rotates the soles of her feet, from a upward- and outward-facing position, so that they are facing inward at the end of the thrust. After completing the thrust, she brings her legs up in line with her body, where they create less drag as she completes her armstroke.

Breathing and Body Position

We will discuss breathing and body position briefly, and then consider some common problems in the following section.

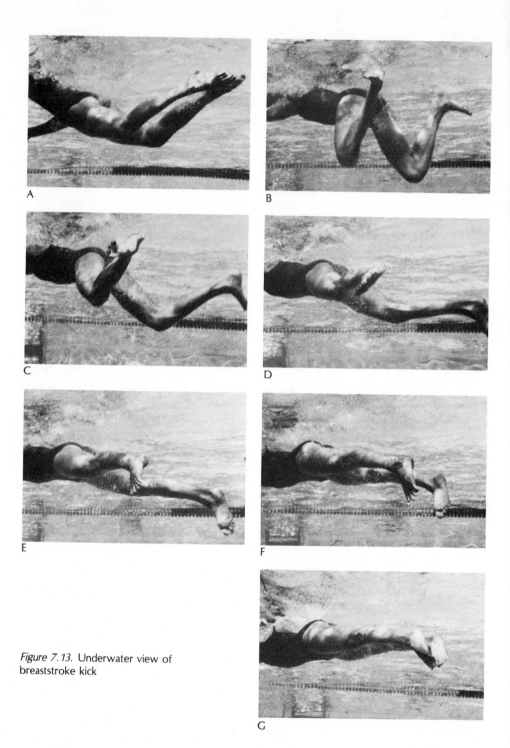

Figure 7.13. Underwater view of breaststroke kick

Breathing. The photographs in Figure 7.14 show the proper breathing technique. Breaststroke swimmers should breathe once during each stroke cycle. That breath is taken as their hands sweep in and up at the completion of the propulsive phase of the armstroke (see Photos B and C).

After taking a breath, lower your face into the water while you recover your arms forward (see Photo D). Keep your face in the water during the outsweep of the armstroke, and exhale slowly during this time (see Photos A and B).

Body Position. Breaststroke swimmers should attempt to maintain their bodies in a streamlined position during as much of each stroke cycle as possible. The ideal body position during the propulsive phase of the armstroke is one in which your legs are held together in an extended position. They should be horizontal with the surface and in line with your trunk. This position is best seen in Photo B of Figure 7.12. Your arms should be close together and extended forward in line with your body during the propulsive phase of the kick (see Photo F of Figure 7.12).

Figure 7.14. Surface view of breaststroke, showing proper breathing

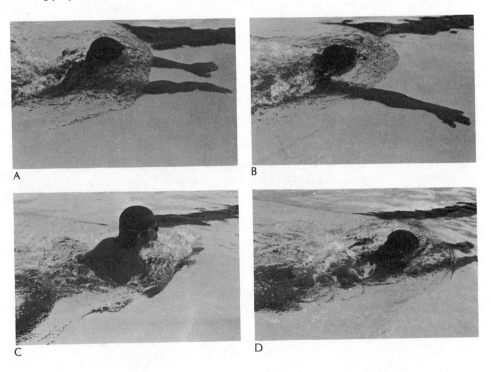

A

B

C

D

The greatest resistance to forward motion occurs during the leg recovery (see Photo D of Figure 7.12). Be sure to recover your legs quickly and gently, with minimal hip flexion, in order to reduce drag during this time.

Some Common Problems

PROBLEM: "It doesn't feel like I'm getting any propulsion from my kick."

SOLUTION: You probably have your feet pointed backward (plantarflexed), rather than outward (dorsiflexed), during the thrust. Be sure to keep your feet dorsiflexed as you kick out and back.

PROBLEM: "My head and shoulders drop underwater during the armstroke."

SOLUTION: You are pulling your hands backward too far under your body during the insweep. Sweep them down and in more, and do not pull them back beyond your shoulders.

PROBLEM: "My arms and legs don't seem to work together."

SOLUTION: You are probably pulling and kicking at the same time. Breaststrokers with weak kicks tend to pull continuously to compensate for the lack of propulsion from their legs. Correct this problem by adding more breaststroke kicking to your workouts. You should also glide for a short time after you complete your kick and before you begin your armstroke.

The Underwater Pullout

Competitive breaststroke swimmers are permitted to stay underwater for one armstroke and one kick after the start of a race and after each turn. Following this underwater stroke, they must bring a portion of their head above the surface of the water and must keep it there until the next turn is made.

You don't need to use this underwater armstroke. However, it is more propulsive than those taken on the surface. Therefore, you will improve your skill as a breaststroke swimmer if you learn the technique for performing it.

The technique for the underwater armstroke is shown in the photographs in Figure 7.15. After pushing off from the wall, the swimmer glides in a streamlined position until he begins to lose speed (see Photo A). He starts the underwater armstroke by sweeping his hands gently outward until the water is behind his arms. The palms of his hands should be facing out and back during this time (see Photo B).

When the water is behind his arms, he sweeps his hands back, down, in, and up until they are under his chest (see Photos B to D). He accom-

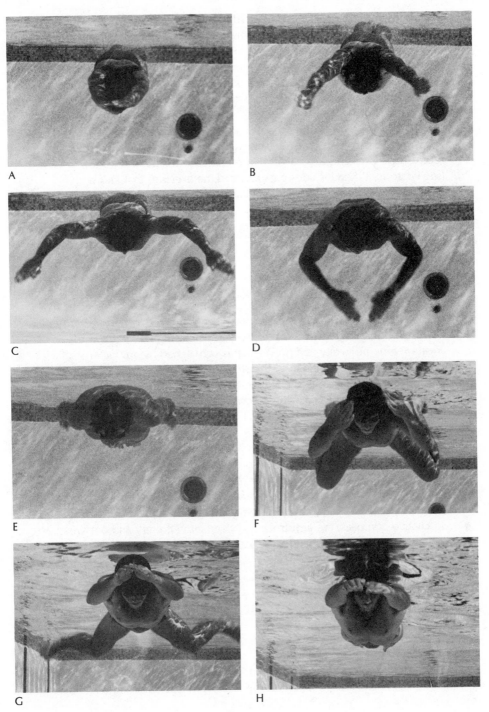

Figure 7.15. Underwater pullout used in breaststroke

plishes this propeller-like sweep by gradually flexing his elbows. He rotates his palms inward and upward during this portion of the underwater armstroke.

When his hands come together under his body, he changes directions abruptly and pushes them backward, outward, and upward toward the surface until his arms are completely extended at his sides (see Photos D and E). The palms of his hands are rotated out and back as he extends his arms.

After completing the underwater armstroke, he glides with his body in a streamlined position until he begins to lose speed (see Photo E). Then, he recovers his arms and legs forward in preparation for the kick to the surface (see Photo F). When his arms pass his head, he executes that kick and reaches for the surface (see Photos G and H).

The Butterfly Stroke

As mentioned earlier, the butterfly is the most difficult stroke to master and probably requires a greater output of energy per length than any of the other strokes we've described. We recommend that you learn it, nevertheless. The butterfly is fun to swim. Once you've mastered it, you will experience a feeling of fluidity and power that is unmatched by any other stroke.

We begin the description of this stroke with the underwater armstroke and the timing of the arms and legs. After that we describe the arm recovery and breathing, and finally the mechanics of the dolphin kick.

Underwater Armstroke

The swimmer in the series of photographs in Figure 7.16 has an excellent armstroke. The best way to visualize the motions she is making is to think of tracing two simultaneous letters "S," one with each hand. This "double S" pattern was illustrated in Figure 6.1 of the preceding chapter. For descriptive purposes, the armstroke is divided into (1) entry and outsweep, (2) insweep, (3) upsweep, and (4) release.

Entry and Outsweep (Photos A to C). The swimmer's hands enter the water just outside shoulder width. Her arms are nearly extended, and the palms of her hands are facing out and back (see Photo B). After entering, her hands sweep gently outward until the water is behind her arms (see Photos B and C). Her palms remain in an outward-facing position.

Insweep (Photos C to G). She begins to apply propulsive force with her arms immediately after she finishes the first downbeat of her kick. She performs the insweep by sweeping her hands backward, downward, inward, and upward under her chest. Her arms are gradually flexed, and the palms of her hands are rotated in and up during this motion.

Upsweep (Photos G to I). When her hands come together under her body, she changes directions and sweeps them out, back, and up toward the surface. Her elbows are gradually extended throughout this movement, and the palms of her hands are rotated to an outward and backward pitch.

Figure 7.16. Front underwater view of butterfly armstroke

A

B

C

D

E

F   (continued)

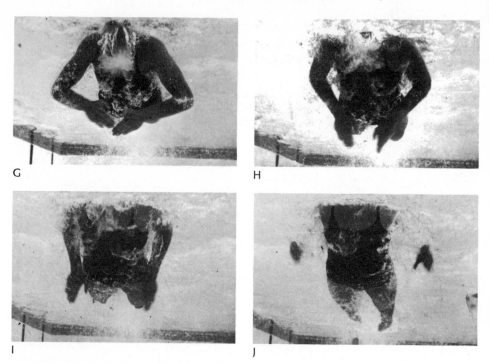

G   H

I   J

Figure 7.16. (continued)

Release (Photo J). She releases the water when her hands reach her thighs, and she turns the palms of her hands inward so they can slice up and out of the water with a minimum of resistance to motion.

Arm Recovery and Breathing

The arm recovery and the inhalation portion of the breathing cycle are shown in the surface photographs in Figure 7.17. We begin with a description of the arm recovery.

Arm Recovery. The swimmer's upper arms come out of the water first, followed by his elbows and hands (see Photos A and B). After releasing the water, he extends his arms and allows their momentum to carry them upward and outward over the water. In this way he can execute the recovery with a minimum of muscular effort.

His arms travel low and laterally over the water until the entry position is reached (see Photos B to D). The palms of his hands remain in the release position throughout the recovery, and the entry is made just outside shoulder width, with the palms of his hands facing outward.

Breathing. The swimmer must begin lifting his head toward the surface during the first half of the underwater armstroke so that his face is out of the water where he can inhale during the second half. His face should break through the surface as his arms meet under his chest, and he should inhale during the final portion of the underwater armstroke and the first half of the arm recovery (see Photos A to C). He should be looking directly forward when he inhales.

His head drops underwater during the second half of the arm recovery (see Photos C and D), and it is completely submerged when his arms enter the water.

Most competitive butterfly swimmers breathe once during every two stroke cycles. (A stroke cycle is one complete armstroke from entry to entry.) You may use this method or you may breathe once during each stroke cycle if you prefer. We recommend against breathing every third or fourth stroke cycle because it is extremely distressing to limit your breathing to this extent. Regardless of the method you use, you must time your exhalation of air so that you will not need air before the next stroke cycle where you intend to breathe.

The Dolphin Kick

Butterfly swimmers kick their legs up and down in unison much like the tail of a dolphin — hence the name that has been given to this kick. One

Figure 7.17. Butterfly arm recovery

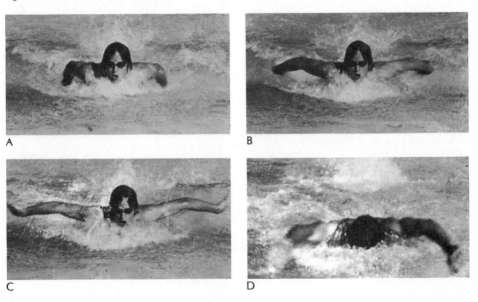

A

B

C

D

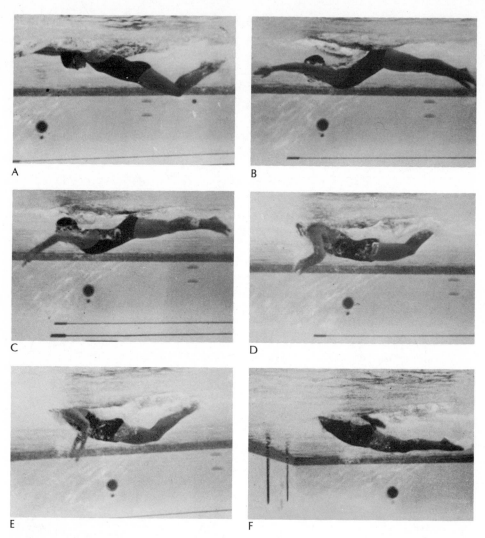

Figure 7.18. Underwater side view of butterfly, showing correct timing of armstroke and kick

complete dolphin kick consists of an upbeat and a downbeat, and, as indicated previously, there are two dolphin kicks per stroke cycle. The mechanics of the dolphin kick are shown from an underwater side view in the series of photographs in Figure 7.18.

We begin with a description of the downbeat:

Downbeat (Photos A, B, D, E, and F). The downbeat of the kick is a simultaneous downward sweep of both legs. Your knees should be flexed slightly when you begin this movement, and your legs should be completely extended when it ends. Your feet should be pointed upward and backward as you begin the downbeat so that backward pressure is applied to the water by the insteps of your feet as they kick downward.

Upbeat (Photos B and C). The swimmer's legs sweep up toward the surface in an extended position. As they near the surface, she begins to flex at the hips and knees in preparation for the next downbeat.

Timing of Arms and Legs

The timing between her armstroke and kick can be seen clearly in Figure 7.18. The downbeat of her first kick occurs as her arms enter the water and sweep outward (see Photos A and B). Her legs recover upward during the insweep of the underwater armstroke (see Photos C and D), and her second downkick occurs during the upsweep (see Photos E and F).

You may have noticed that her first and second kicks are not identical. The downbeat of her second kick, shown in Photos D to F, is not as long or deep as the first downkick. On the other hand, her first downkick is considerably longer and pushes her hips higher. This does not mean, as some have theorized, that swimmers should put more effort into the first kick. You should put an equal amount of effort in both kicks. These differences result from changes in body position during the two kicks rather than variations in effort. She is reaching forward and down when she executes the first downkick, so, quite naturally, it causes her hips to rise higher. On the other hand, her head and shoulders are up during the second downkick, which inhibits both the length of her kick and the amount by which her hips rise.

Some Common Problems

PROBLEM: "My arms drag through the water during the recovery."

SOLUTION: Try swinging your arms higher over the water. If you are unable to do this, you may need to improve your shoulder flexibility. The shoulder flexibility exercises described in Chapter 3 can help in this respect.

PROBLEM: "I only kick once during each stroke cycle."

SOLUTION: You are probably pulling your hands backward too rapidly during the underwater armstroke. Pulling in nearly a straight backward direction will cause you to complete your underwater armstroke so quickly that there is not enough time to kick twice before your hands leave the water. Exaggerate the outward and inward sweeps of your hands during the first two-thirds of the underwater armstroke. This gives you enough time to get your legs in position for the missing kick.

PROBLEM: "I can't seem to keep my legs from sinking when I swim butterfly."

SOLUTION: You may have a one-kick butterfly, in which case you correct it by using the solution described in the previous section. On the other hand, your problem may stem from the fact that you lose some of the force from your kick because you do not have enough ankle flexibility to kick properly. Use some of the plantarflexing stretching exercises described in Chapter 3 to increase the range of motion in these joints.

The Turn Used for Butterfly and Breaststroke

Butterfly and breaststroke swimmers turn in a similar manner. The only differences occur after they leave the wall. Breaststroke swimmers use the long underwater armstroke and glide that was described earlier, while butterfly swimmers kick to the surface after a shorter glide.

A butterfly swimmer is shown performing the turn in the series of photographs in Figure 7.19. In Photos A and B, he has grasped the lip of the gutter with both hands and is pulling his legs forward into the wall. He does this by flexing his arms and legs. His legs are tucked tightly to increase their speed into the wall.

Next, he removes his left hand and slides it backward, using only his right arm to continue pulling his legs into the wall (see Photo C). As his feet near the wall, he removes his right hand and carries it over the water with a high elbow in the manner of a front crawl arm recovery. He then slices it down into the water, where it meets his left hand above his head (see Photos D and E). In the meantime he has turned the palm of his left hand upward, and he pushes it up against the water to aid in pulling his head down.

When his feet reach the wall, they are planted with toes pointed sideward and knees flexed approximately 90 degrees (see Photo E). His hands are together overhead, and his body is aligned for the pushoff.

He pushes off the wall on his side and rotates to a face-down position during the glide that follows (see Photos E to G). He glides in a streamlined position until he begins to lose speed. Then, if swimming butterfly, he executes two or three dolphin kicks and one armstroke. These bring his head to the surface, where he can begin swimming butterfly. If the swimmer in these photographs had been swimming breaststroke he would push off somewhat deeper and execute an underwater armstroke before kicking to the surface.

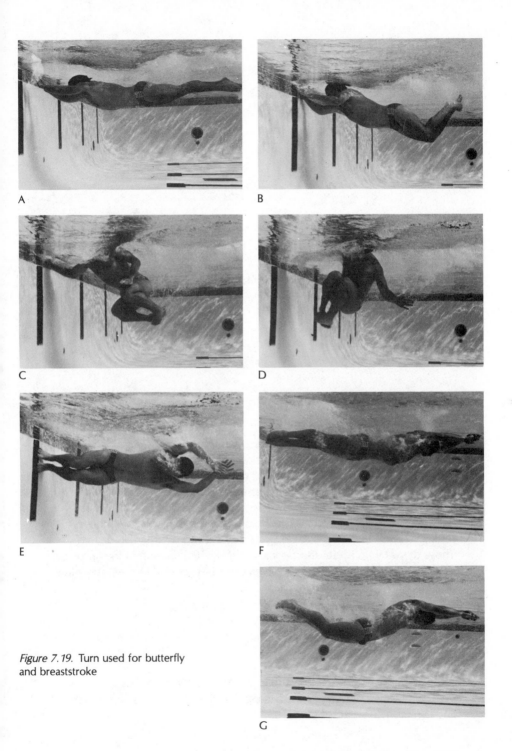

A

B

C

D

E

F

G

Figure 7.19. Turn used for butterfly
and breaststroke

The Noncompetitive Strokes

Three of the strokes that are not swum in competition are described in this chapter: the sidestroke, the overarm sidestroke, and the elementary backstroke. As indicated earlier, they are all resting strokes because they incorporate a short glide or resting phase at the end of each cycle. These strokes are not, under normal conditions, as vigorous as the competitive strokes. Nevertheless, some of you may feel more comfortable swimming these resting strokes, and for this reason you may wish to use them in training. Those of you who prefer the resting strokes should know that they provide an adequate training effect if you swim them fast enough to meet the intensity requirements described in Chapter 2.

The Sidestroke

The mechanics of the sidestroke are described in the following sequence: (1) body position and breathing, (2) armstroke and timing of arms and legs, and (3) scissors kick.

A   B

Figure 8.1. Side and top views of sidestroke,
showing correct gliding position

Body Position and Breathing

The photographs in Figure 8.1 show the correct body position for the
sidestroke. Photo A shows the correct horizontal alignment, while Photo B
shows the correct lateral alignment.

The swimmer is in the glide phase of her stroke in both photographs.
The correct horizontal alignment is with her arms outstretched near the surface. Her bottom arm, the one deepest in the water, is extended forward;
the top arm, the one nearest the surface, is extended behind her. Her legs
are extended and held together near the surface. There is a slight incline
from her head to her feet, which is unavoidable in this stroke. The swimmer
in Photo A has reduced it to a minimum.

The position of her head is probably the most important factor in maintaining good horizontal alignment. Her cheek is in the water even though
most of her face is out of the water (see Photo B). If her head were completely out of the water, her hips and legs would sink even more in order
to compensate for the weight being held above the surface.

Breathing is no problem in this stroke. Since you are on your side with
your mouth above the surface, you can inhale and exhale at any point
during the stroke cycle.

Armstroke and Timing of Arms and Legs

The series of photographs in Figure 8.2 show the sidestroke armstroke
and the timing of the arms and legs from a front underwater view. One
complete stroke cycle begins and ends with a glide (see Photos A and H).
The arms stroke alternately, with the bottom arm applying propulsive force
as the swimmer sweeps them toward her chest (see Photos B to E). Her top
arm applies propulsive force as they return to their extended positions.

A   B

C   D

Figure 8.2. Underwater front view of
sidestroke armstroke

  The swimmer begins her bottom armstroke by pressing gently downward and slightly outward until the water is behind her arm (see Photo B).
Once the catch is made, she applies propulsive force by sweeping her hand
in a half-circle that is downward, backward, upward, and inward (see
Photos C, D, and E). The propulsive phase of the bottom armstroke ends as
her hand reaches her chest (see Photo E). She accomplishes this sweep by
gradually flexing her elbow and adducting her arm (pushing it down toward
her side). The palm of her hand should rotate from a backward- and slightly
outward-facing position at the beginning of the sweep, to an inward- and
upward-facing position as her hand reaches her chest.

  Her top arm recovers while her bottom arm is propelling her body forward. She accomplishes this recovery by flexing her elbow and sliding that
arm gently forward along her side until it reaches her chest (see Photos
C to E).

  The propulsive phase of the top armstroke begins when both arms
meet at her chest (see Photo E). She sweeps her top arm from her chest to
her thigh in another half-circle path. It travels down, out, back, up, and in

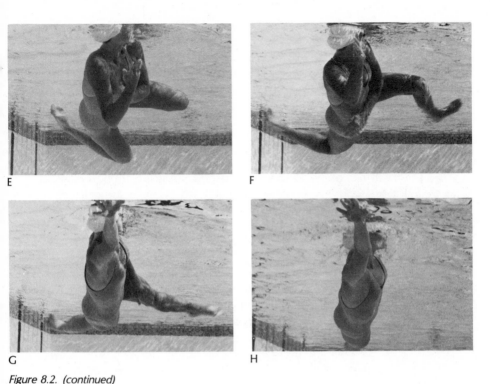

E   F

G   H

Figure 8.2. (continued)

until her hand is resting palm down on the side of her thigh (see Photos F to H). The palm of her hand is facing backward and slightly outward during the first half of this sweep, and it faces backward and inward during the second half. The propulsive phase of her top armstroke is accomplished by gradually extending her arm at the elbow.

She gently recovers her bottom arm forward while she sweeps her top arm to her thigh (see Photos F to H). She reaches forward until it is completely extended overhead, parallel with and just beneath the surface of the water (see Photo H).

In Figure 8.2, the timing of the swimmer's arms and legs is not completely accurate. Her legs should be held close together in an extended position just under the surface of the water during most of the propulsive phase of the bottom armstroke (see Photos B to D), and she should not begin recovering her legs forward until the time when her hands near her chest in Photo F. Her timing is correct for the remainder of the stroke cycle.

Once her legs have been recovered, she stretches them out into an open scissors position during the first half of the top armstroke (see Photos

F and G). She squeezes them together during the final half of that armstroke (see Photos G and H).

After completing one stroke cycle, she glides for a short time before starting the next cycle (see Photos H and A). A simple way to remember the correct timing of the arms and legs is to squeeze your legs together as you extend your arms.

The Scissors Kick

The mechanics of the scissors kick are shown from a rear underwater view in Figure 8.3. The swimmer is gliding in Photo A. During the glide her legs are held together in an extended position, and her toes are pointed backward. Her legs ride just below the surface and are nearly parallel with it. This position of the legs minimizes drag so that the speed of the glide can be maintained for a longer time.

The leg recovery is shown in Photo B. The swimmer brings her legs forward by flexing at both the hips and the knees. Her legs should be held close together as they are brought gently forward. This minimizes the increase in drag that unavoidably accompanies this leg recovery.

She begins to apply propulsive force with her top leg (the leg nearest the surface), when her feet near her buttocks. At that time, she extends her top leg outward and backward. Her foot is in a flat (dorsiflexed) position so that she is applying force with the sole (see Photos C to E). In the meantime, she stretches her bottom leg behind her with her knee flexed more than 90 degrees and her foot pointed backward (plantarflexed). She applies propulsive force by squeezing her legs inward until they are together (see Photos E to G). Her top leg remains completely extended during the inward squeeze, while her bottom leg is gradually extended at the knee. When the inward squeeze is performed correctly, you should feel that you are applying pressure with the back of your top leg and the sole of that foot while pressure should be felt on the front of your bottom leg and the instep of that foot. After completing the inward squeeze, she holds her legs together in an extended position and glides until she begins to lose speed (see Photo G).

The Inverted Scissors Kick

Some swimmers prefer to extend their top leg backward when they use the scissors kick. This style has become known as the *inverted* scissors kick, for obvious reasons. Both styles are equally effective, in most cases. Try both, and choose the one you prefer.

The recovery is similar in both styles. The difference occurs as your legs

Figure 8.3. Underwater rear view of the scissors kick

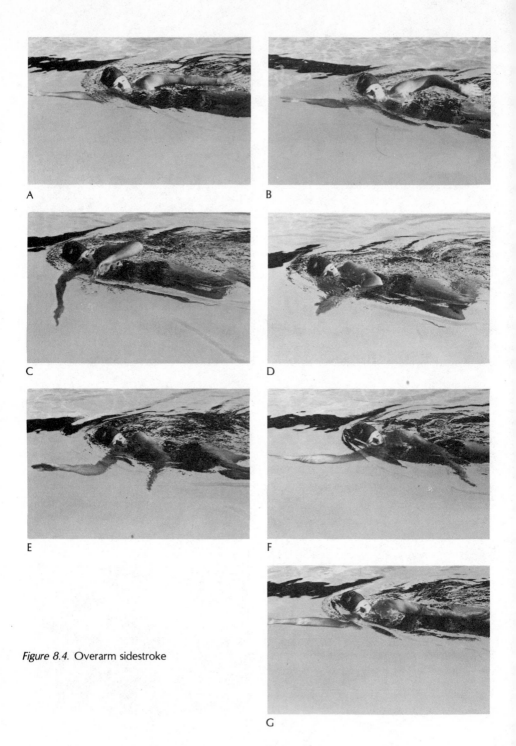

Figure 8.4. Overarm sidestroke

are extended outward. In the inverted scissors kick, the top leg is extended back in a flexed position while the bottom leg is stretched forward in an extended position. When your legs are squeezed together, you extend your top leg and apply force with the front of that leg and the instep of that foot. Your bottom leg squeezes inward in an extended position with force applied by the back of that leg and the sole of that foot.

The Overarm Sidestroke

A surface view of the overarm sidestroke is shown in Figure 8.4. It is identical to the sidestroke in all respects except that, as we mentioned, the top arm is recovered over rather than through the water. That recovery is shown in Photos B to D of Figure 8.4. The overarm sidestroke is a more efficient and faster version of the sidestroke because the overwater recovery reduces drag on the top arm as it is brought forward to your chest.

We describe one stroke cycle, emphasizing the recovery of the top arm. After gliding in a streamlined position (see Photo A), the swimmer begins to stroke with her bottom arm. At the same time she brings her top arm forward over the water in a manner that is very similar to the high-elbow recovery used in the front crawl stroke. Her top arm is brought forward over the water by gradually flexing her elbow (see Photos B and C). Once that hand passes her chest, she reaches forward and slices it down into the water to meet her other hand at a point that is just in front of her chest (see Photo D). She then sweeps her top arm backward while recovering her bottom arm forward (see Photos E to G).

Some Common Problems

Due to their similarity, the same problems sometimes occur when swimming either the sidestroke or overarm sidestroke. Therefore, these problems are discussed together here.

PROBLEM: "My head drops underwater when I swim these strokes."

SOLUTION: You are probably sweeping both arms back at the same time and then pushing your head under as you recover them forward simultaneously. You can correct this problem by gliding longer at the end of each stroke cycle. This counteracts the tendency to stroke too quickly with your bottom arm.

PROBLEM: "My kick seems to slow me down."

SOLUTION: You are probably recovering your legs incorrectly. That is, you are keeping them extended and pushing them outward and forward. Be sure to bend your legs during the recovery. Slide them forward by gently flexing at the knees and hips.

PROBLEM: "My hips and legs sink when I swim these strokes."

SOLUTION: You are probably holding your head completely out of the water when you swim, and your feet and hips are sinking to compensate for the weight of your head. Be certain that one side of your face is underwater. When part of your face is in the water, some of your head's weight is supported, and your hips and legs ride nearer the surface.

The Elementary Backstroke

The elementary backstroke is one of the easiest, if not the easiest, stroke to master. It is a stroke that novice swimmers can use to build up their aerobic endurance until they have mastered some of the more complex strokes we described in Chapter 7.

In describing this stroke, we mention two techniques that are not commonly taught. We believe these techniques permit a more effective application of propulsive force. The first is a bent-arm underwater stroke. Most manuals recommend that your arms be kept extended as they stroke through the water, although the most recent edition of the American Red Cross Swimming and Water Safety Manual states that either the bent-arm or straight-arm technique can be used.

The second technique is an asynchronous timing of the arms and legs. The term *asynchronous timing* refers to the fact that the kick is completed before the propulsive phase of the armstroke begins. The timing of this stroke has traditionally been taught with arms and legs applying propulsive force simultaneously. Asynchronous timing should be more efficient because the propulsive phases of the arms and legs are separated, as they are in most of the other strokes. Kicking during the final stages of the arm recovery should reduce the decelerative effects of that recovery. The elementary backstroke will be described in the following sections: (1) body position, (2) armstroke, (3) kick, and (4) timing of arms and legs.

Body Position

The swimmer in the photograph in Figure 8.5 displays excellent horizontal alignment. The back of her head is in the water so that a portion of its weight is supported. Her hips are near the surface. Her legs are extended, near the surface and parallel with it. Her feet are pointed backward to reduce drag.

Figure 8.5. Underwater side view of elementary backstroke, showing good horizontal alignment

She "breaks" from this streamlined position when she recovers her legs. The break should be gentle and minimal, however. She lowers her hips and flexes her legs at the hips and knees. The horizontal body position pictured in Figure 8.5 should be resumed during the second half of the armstroke and during the glide that follows.

Recovery and Armstroke

The elementary backstroke armstroke is illustrated by the swimmer in the sequence of photographs in Figure 8.6. It will be described in two sections: (1) recovery and (2) armstroke.

Recovery (Photos A to C). In Photo A, she begins to recover her arms (and legs) after a short glide. She slides her hands forward along her body by gradually flexing at the elbows. She begins reaching overhead as her hands pass her shoulders (see Photo B). She completes the recovery by extending her arms forward and outward until they are completely straight and just outside her shoulders (see Photo C).

Armstroke (Photos D to F). She begins the armstroke by pressing outward and downward until the water is behind her arms (see Photo D). The catch is made, and the propulsive phase begins at that point. The palms of her hands should be facing out and back during this time.

She sweeps her hands backward, upward, and inward, gradually bending her arms until they are flexed nearly 90 degrees (see Photo E). The palms of her hands are rotated in and up as she flexes her arms.

Next, she extends her arms in a backward, downward, and inward direction until they are completely straight and in contact with her body (see Photo F). Her palms are gradually rotated down and in as she extends her arms.

Following the completion of this armstroke, she glides for a short time

Figure 8.6. Underwater front view of elementary backstroke armstroke

before beginning another stroke cycle. Drag can be reduced during the glide by holding your extended arms against your sides with your palms resting against your thighs.

Kick

A rear underwater view of the kick is shown in Figure 8.7. The kick that is used in this stroke is almost identical to the breaststroke kick except,

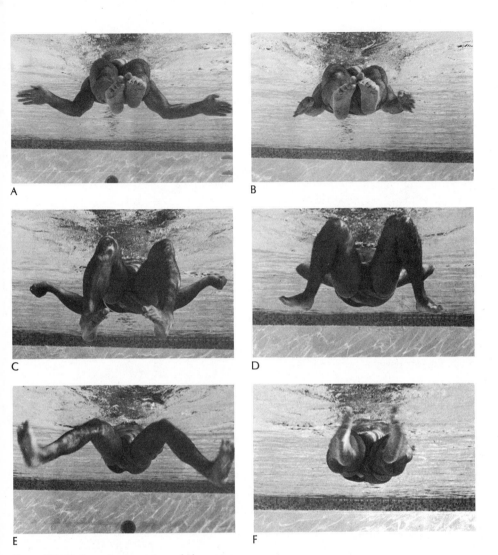

Figure 8.7. Underwater rear view of elementary backstroke kick

of course, that the swimmer is on her back. We describe it in the following sections: (1) glide, (2) recovery, (3) outsweep, and (4) insweep.

Glide (Photo A). The swimmer holds her legs in a completely extended position during the glide. They are close together, with her toes pointed backward to reduce drag. Her legs should be parallel with and just beneath the surface.

Recovery (Photos B and C). She recovers her legs gently downward and forward by flexing at the knees. Her knees separate but are no farther apart than shoulder width during the recovery. Her feet remain inside her knees to reduce drag. She must not flex her legs excessively at the hip, or her knees will come out of the water.

Outsweep (Photos D and E). The propulsive phase of the kick begins as her feet pass directly below her knees. At that time, she begins to extend her legs, and she circles her feet out, up, and back. The soles of her feet should be facing out and back in a dorsiflexed position, and she applies force with the inside of her legs and the soles of her feet.

Insweep (Photos E and F). When her legs are completely extended and at their widest point, she squeezes them inward across the water until they come together. The soles of her feet should be facing in during this phase of the kick. A technique that will help you achieve the correct pitch during the insweep is to touch the soles of your feet together as you complete the kick.

Figure 8.8. Top view of elementary backstroke, showing timing of arms and legs

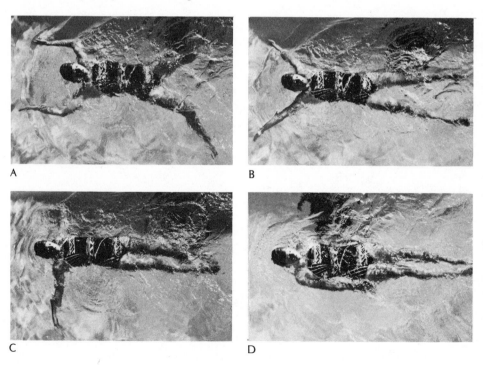

A

B

C

D

Timing of Arms and Legs

The asynchronous timing of the arms and legs that we recommend is shown in the photographs in Figure 8.8. After gliding, the swimmer recovers her arms and legs. Her leg recovery is completed during the first half of the arm recovery, and she begins the propulsive phase of her kick as her arms extend overhead (see Photos A and B). After the kick is completed, she sweeps her arms down to her sides (see Photos C and D). When the propulsive phase of the armstroke is finished, she glides for a short time before beginning the next stroke cycle.

Some Common Problems

PROBLEM: "I don't seem to get any propulsion from my kick."

SOLUTION: You are probably pointing your toes backward as you kick. Be sure to keep your feet flat with your soles facing out during the outsweep.

PROBLEM: "My hips sink when I recover my legs."

SOLUTION: You are flexing your legs too much at the hips as you recover them. You probably pull your thighs up and forward, which, in turn, causes your hips to sink. If your knees are breaking the surface as you recover your legs, this is the cause of your problem. To correct it, recover your legs by bending at the knees. Don't pull your thighs up.

PROBLEM: "My face goes underwater when I recover my arms."

SOLUTION: You are probably bringing your arms out of the water as you recover them forward. Their weight causes a counterforce that submerges your head. Be sure to keep your arms underwater throughout the entire recovery, particularly as your hands pass your shoulders.

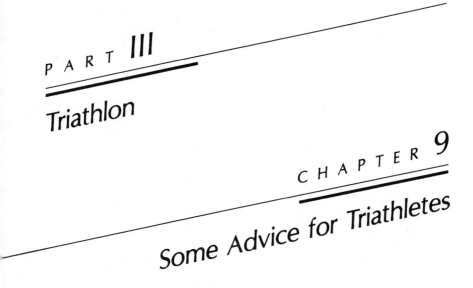

Triathlon

CHAPTER 9

Some Advice for Triathletes

The triathlon is the newest of the "marathon" events — some say it is the fastest growing sport in the world. It is really three events in one. One person completes, for distance, a swim, a bicycle ride, and a run. The distances are preset by the meet committee. The three events are completed in sequence, with no rest between each. Placement is determined by the total time the athlete requires to finish all the events.

The triathlon has caused a surge of interest in swimming among people who normally restrict their exercise to land events. Most of us have spent a great deal of time running and cycling since childhood, so we are reasonably proficient in these skills. In addition, since both sports require well-conditioned legs, most runners can compete well in cycling and vice versa. Unfortunately, many triathletes flounder when it comes to swimming because they've used this skill less over the years and because swimming is an arms-dominated sport. These people reason (and rightly so) that they can improve their performances most by concentrating on the weakest of their three skills.

An advantageous by-product of this interest in swim training has been a reduction in training-related injuries. Some triathletes are finding that they can substitute swim training for some of their running mileage without losing any circulatory and respiratory training effects. As a result, they are experiencing fewer joint and muscle injuries. To those of you who are now training for the triathlon or are interested in trying the sport, we offer the following advice for training and competing in the swimming portion of this event.

Swimming the Race

To begin with, you should develop a good front crawl stroke. It is the fastest stroke, and if you expect to be competitive you should become proficient with it. Some of you may be using the breaststroke, sidestroke, or elementary backstroke because you lack the skill to swim the front crawl for the entire race distance. If you are in this category, you should spend more of your training time swimming the front crawl, and you should learn to swim it for long distances. Keep reminding yourself that people have swum the English Channel and farther using only the front crawl stroke. After a few weeks or months of training, you'll realize that it is not only possible, but preferable, to use this stroke in your races.

Use the description of the front crawl stroke in Chapter 7 to help you perfect your mechanics. Pay particular attention to the information on breathing. You must learn to breathe as comfortably and economically while swimming as you breathe when running or cycling. Learn to inhale and exhale normally by rolling your head to the side once during each stroke cycle. Don't gasp for air or hold your breath for three or four arm cycles before taking your next breath.

Concentrate on developing a rhythmic, comfortable stroke rate that is compatible with conserving energy over long distances. It is best to use a slightly shorter and less powerful armstroke and to recover your arms over the water with an inertial motion that requires minimal effort. The small amount of speed you lose early in a race is more than offset by the savings in energy, and you will be able to swim the later portions of the race at a considerably faster pace.

We also recommend that you reduce the effort you expend in kicking. Use leg movements that are designed to stabilize rather than to propel your body. Kicking requires a lot of energy because of the many large leg muscles that are used. On the other hand, kicking adds very little to one's speed. For this reason, the two-beat, two-beat crossover, or four-beat rhythms are preferable to a traditional six-beat kick. The reduced number of leg beats conserves energy and enables one to swim longer at an average faster pace.

If, despite our advice, you prefer a six-beat rhythm, use a "light" effort.

Kick gently, using the least amount of effort that can keep your legs afloat and your body aligned.

There is a drill that can help you find the proper kicking effort for swimming long distances. Swim several lengths of the pool, kicking easier and lighter on each length until, on one particular length, your body begins to wiggle or your legs will no longer remain afloat. Either of these reactions indicates that you are kicking below the minimum effort needed to maintain alignment. Put just a little more effort into your kick on the next length, and that will be the proper kicking effort for your stroke.

Although most swimmers breathe to only one side, you should become proficient at breathing to either side. This allows you to "keep an eye" on competitors who are swimming on either side. A swimmer who always breathes to the same side may lose track of contestants who are swimming on his or her "blind side." You can learn this skill by practicing the alternate breathing technique for the front crawl stroke (Chapter 7). Use alternate breathing occasionally in practice until you can breathe comfortably to either side. What we have just said does not contradict our advice to breathe once during each stroke cycle when competing. In races, it is only necessary to breathe alternately when you want to check on the position of your competition. At other times, you should breathe during every stroke cycle.

Navigation can be a problem when swimming in open water. One recommendation for racing is that you learn to swim with your face out of the water. This technique should be used occasionally to "spot" where you are going. It is more fatiguing to swim with your face out of, rather than in, the water. That is why you should swim with your head up for only a few strokes at a time. Before the beginning of the race, select some landmarks that can help you navigate a straight course through the open water. These may be a buoy, a boat, a tower, or some other floating object that you can swim toward. In the absence of floating markers, pick some object on the far shore that is easily spotted. During the race, look up once every eight or so strokes to determine if you are on course. You can reduce the number of times you raise your head out of the water by "staying with the pack" and by using alternate breathing or simply watching the other swimmers underwater. Allow them to steer your course until you are the leader and must steer it for yourself. And, finally, it goes without saying that you should wear goggles during your races.

There are two training techniques that will help you become accustomed to swimming with your face out of the water. The first is to swim some occasional 25-, 50- and even 100-yard/meter repeats with your head out of the water. The second, and probably the better, training drill is to lift your face out of the water for a stroke or two, once every eight or ten strokes during some of your repeat sets.

In addition to navigation, two other problems are peculiar to racing in open water. Lake and ocean water is usually colder than pool water. There-fore, preserving heat becomes an important consideration. In addition, swimmers are subject to chafing during prolonged exposure to open water.

Heat loss can be a major problem. Most pools are maintained at tem-peratures that are between 78° and 84° F (25° and 28° C), while the temperatures of lakes and oceans are frequently below 70° F (20° C). Hy-pothermia (excessively lowered body temperature) can occur when a swim-mer is exposed to low temperatures for a long period of time. The effort you expend racing produces heat, which decreases the likelihood of hypothermia. Nevertheless, you would be wise to wear a swim cap when you train and race in open water. People lose approximately 30 percent of their body heat from the tops of their heads. A swim cap helps pre-serve your body heat and may help you swim longer and faster in cold water. Another safeguard against hypothermia is to cover most of your body with a heat-preserving grease. Several different brands are sold commercially.

The use of a grease product or Vaseline will also prevent chafing, a common problem in long swims, particularly in salt water. Apply the prod-uct under your armpits where your arms come in contact with your "lats" (sides) as you stroke. It is also a good idea to put some lubricant under the seams of your swimsuit where they are likely to rub against your skin. For men, the areas are the thighs, groin, and waist. Women should also put Vaseline under their shoulder straps, around the neck line, and across the lower back where the seams of their suits may chafe.

A final recommendation comes from Dave Scott, three-time winner of the Ironman trophy, the most prestigious event in triathlon. He suggests that triathletes should use the breaststroke for the final 10 to 15 yards of the swimming event. This accustoms the hamstrings and dorsiflexors of the legs and ankles to the pedaling motions that are used in the cycling event that follows. These muscles are used very little in the flutter kick. He reasons, therefore, that swimming breaststroke just before leaving the water will have a warm-up effect that may discourage cramps in the hamstrings and calves during the land events.

Training for the Race

The first question that most triathletes ask is "Will it do me any good to train in a pool if I'm going to race in rough water?" The answer is yes. Pools offer the advantage of a structured environment for systematic interval training. You can swim multiples of a known distance with a pace clock to provide a means for controlling your rest intervals and determining your repeat speeds. The motivation and control of this framework build aerobic endurance at the fastest possible rate, perhaps faster than it could be improved by lake or ocean swimming for undetermined distances at unknown speeds.

However, lake and ocean training help you adjust your pace to the increased energy cost of swimming in rough water. You learn to use markers for navigation, and you can acclimatize to the colder water. So you build aerobic endurance by training frequently in swimming pools, and you learn to use that endurance in races by training occasionally in open water.

Structure your training program according to the information we provided in Chapters 2 and 3. Of course, the frequency and duration of your training sessions depend on the time you have available. However, for best results, you should swim four or five days per week. Three days of swim training per week is the absolute minimum, if you are a serious competitor.

The swimming portions of triathlons are at least a quarter mile in length, and for some major events they may exceed two miles. Unfortunately, we cannot cite optimum daily training yardages that will prepare you for these various race distances. The issue of optimum yardage has yet to be resolved in the sport of competitive swimming. There is no research to guide us in this matter, and experiential information is contradictory. Successful competitive swimmers who specialize in races that are approximately one mile in length have trained with as "little" as 8,000 yards/meters per day and as "much" as 30,000 yards/meters per day.

You can see, therefore, that we are not being excessive when we recommend that triathletes should swim a minimum of 2,000 to 4,000 yards/meters at each training session. High-level athletes who compete in the longer swims may want to increase these amounts to between 5,000 and 8,000 yards/meters per session. Depending on your swimming skill, it takes approximately one hour to complete 2,500 to 4,000 yards/meters, and it should take two hours to swim between 5,000 and 8,000 yards/meters.

The next topic concerns the types of repeat sets that you should use in training. Although we stated earlier that you can improve aerobic endurance by swimming any repeat distance on a short rest interval, triathletes are best advised to spend most of their training time swimming longer repeats. Repeat distances of 400 yards/meters have the "feel" of races. They require similar stroking rates, and they encourage you to find a comfortable rhythm.

It is also a good idea to swim long sets of repeats; that is, sets that include a large number of repeats. Try to structure your sets so that they require a minimum of 20 minutes to complete. The maximum time may be one hour or more.

Keep your rest intervals as short as possible, even shorter than those that we recommended for fitness swimmers. Shorter rest intervals guide you into swimming at a steady, moderate pace that is ideal for improving aerobic endurance. With shorter rest intervals, you are also able to complete more distance in less time during your training session. Take 5 to 10 seconds rest on "short" repeats of 100 to 300 yards/meters. Keep your rest intervals between 15 and 30 seconds for the longer repeat distances (400 yards/meters and longer).

Maintain your training intensity at the moderate level we've recommended for improving aerobic endurance. Use your repeat speeds, heart rate, breathing rate, or sensations of perceived exertion to monitor the correct intensity. Put special emphasis on swimming all your repeats at an even pace. Try to maintain the same speed for each of the repeats in a set. If you plan to "go for it" on any repeat, make that repeat the last one of the set.

Even though middle-distance repeats should be used most frequently in training, we also recommend the occasional use of shorter repeat distances and long continuous swims. Shorter repeat distances improve your speed. They should be done about once each week. The best repeat distances are 50 yards/meters and 100 yards/meters. Use short rest intervals. The shorter distances encourage an increase in repeat speed. You do not need to provide more rest for this purpose. More rest would encourage a shift away from aerobic toward anaerobic metabolism. With more rest you will tend to swim so fast that you will need to go into debt for oxygen. Lactic acid will accumulate, and fatigue will force you to reduce your training yardage below amounts that are optimum for improving your aerobic endurance.

Triathletes who are competing in swimming events one mile or more in length should swim some long-distance repeats at least once each week. Twice per week would be preferable. We suggest repeat distances of 800 yards/meters to 2,000 yards/meters. They accustom you to swimming continuously for long periods of time. A long continuous swim that is equal to or up to twice the length of the race distance is also good for this purpose. One such swim should be completed every week or two.

Some competitive swimmers and coaches are prejudiced against long continuous swims. They consider such swims too slow-paced and boring and do not recommend them for these reasons. You should remember, however, that most competitive swimmers do not compete in races that are more than a quarter mile in length. When your competitions involve continuous swims of one mile or more, it makes good sense to train with these distances occasionally. A straight four-mile swim may seem to be "cruel and unusual punishment," but it can be completed in only 60 to 90 minutes. Most triathletes would think nothing of running or cycling continuously for this length of time. Why not swimming?

Try to swim in open water at least once every week or two, weather permitting. Complete one or more long continuous swims, preferably race distance or longer on those days. Some of the swims can be at a moderate pace, and some of them should be at race pace. Serious competitors should swim a race distance "time trial" at least once every three weeks (but not within two weeks of the race).

It is always advisable to have a friend accompany you with a boat when you attempt open-water swims. It is easy to "veer off course," and the tides and undertow can be treacherous in places.

Suggested Readings

1. Adams, W. C., McHenry, M. M., and Bernauer, E. M. Long-Term Physiologic Adaptations to Exercise with Specific Reference to Performance and Cardio-respiratory Function in Health and Disease. In E. A. Amsterdam, J. H. Wilmore, and A. N. DeMario (eds.), *Exercise in Cardiovascular Health and Disease*, pp. 322–343. New York: Yorke Medical Books, 1977.
2. Astrand, P. O., and Rodahl, K. *Textbook of Work Physiology.* New York: McGraw-Hill, 1977.
3. Brems, M. *Swim for Fitness.* San Francisco: Chronicle Books, 1979.
4. Counsilman, J. E. *The Complete Book of Swimming.* New York: Atheneum, 1978.
5. Fox, E. L., and Mathews, D. K. *The Physiological Basis of Physical Education and Athletics.* Philadelphia: Saunders, 1981.
6. Katz, J., with Bruning, N. P. *Swimming for Total Fitness.* New York: Doubleday, 1981.
7. Lamb, D. R. *Physiology of Exercise: Responses and Adaptations.* New York: Macmillan, 1978.
8. Maglischo, E. W. *Swimming Faster.* Palo Alto, Calif.: Mayfield, 1982.
9. McArdle, W. D., Katch, F. I., and Katch, B. L. *Exercise Physiology: Energy, Nutrition and Human Performance.* Philadelphia: Lea & Febiger, 1981.
10. Pollock, M. L., Wilmore, J. H., and Fox, S. M., III. *Health and Fitness Through Physical Activity.* New York: Wiley, 1978.

Sample Log

This is an example of how to use a log to keep track of your training. The log on the next page may be photocopied and used for recordkeeping.

Day Monday Date Sept. 3, 1984		Departure Times	Average Speed	Heart Rate, Breathing Rate, or Perceived Effort Rating
Warm-up	200 swim			140
Main series	10 × 100 front crawl	1:45	1:15	155
Kicking set	300 breaststroke		5:15	150
Pulling or sprint set	2 × 500	7:00	6:30	160
Cool-down	200			
Comments	Reduce the departure time for 100's to 1:30 next time			

Day Date	Departure Times	Average Speed	Heart Rate, Breathing Rate, or Perceived Effort Rating
Warm-up			
Main series			
Kicking set			
Pulling or sprint set			
Cool-down			
Comments			

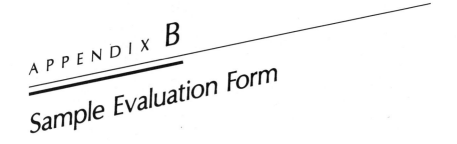

APPENDIX B
Sample Evaluation Form

Name: Age: Class:

	Date	Test 1	Date	Test 2	Date	Test 3
Percentage of body fat						
Body girth measurements Right calf						
Left calf						
Right thigh						
Left thigh						
Hips						
Waist						
Chest (bust)						
Right bicep						
Left bicep						
Resting heart rate						
Working heart rate						
Recovery rate						

Your computed maximum heart
rate at work:

Your computed working rate at
70% of maximum:

220 − your age = maximum heart rate at work

220 − _____ = _____

220 − your age × .70 = 70% of your maximum

220 − _____ × .70 = _____

Your body weight in pounds: Test 1 Date: Test 2 Date: Test 3 Date:

    _____   _____   _____

APPENDIX C
Swimming Supply Companies

1. Finals — Primarily suits and caps — 21 Minisink Ave.
Port Jervis, NY 12771

2. Kiefer McNeil — General supplies — 910 Lake Road
Medina, OH 44258

3. Competitive Aquatic Supply — General supplies — 4134 South Street
Lakewood, CA 90714

4. The Swim Shop — General supplies — 1400 8th Ave. So.
PO Box 1402
Nashville, TN 37203

5. World Wide Aquatics — General supplies — 509 Wyoming Ave.
Cincinnati, OH 45215

6. Kast-A-Way Swim Wear — Primarily suits — 9356 Cincinnati/Columbus Rd.
Cincinnati, OH 45241

7. Metro Swim Shop — General supplies — PO Box 156
Dept. SW 982
Berkeley Heights, NJ 07922

8. Swimmer's Supply — General supplies — 3118 Beach Blvd.
Jacksonville, FL 32207
or
7286 SW 40th St.
Miami, FL 33155

9. Uglies	General supplies	1617 E. Highland Phoenix, AZ 85016 *or* 6121 E. Broadway Tucson, AZ 85711
10. South Swim	General supplies	2706 Chapel Hill Blvd. Durham, NC 27707
11. TJ's	General supplies	577 Route 46 Kenvil, NJ 07847
12. Aquaforum Training Films	Films: 16 mm, super 8 mm, and cassette	PO Box 84 Willsboro, NJ 12996
13. Swim Gear	General supplies	207 Main Street Huntington Beach, CA 92683

References

Adams, W. C., McHenry, M. M., and Bernauer, E. M. Long-term physiologic adaptations to exercise with specific reference to performance and cardiorespiratory function in health and disease. In E. A. Amsterdam, J. H. Wilmore, and A. N. DeMario (eds.), *Exercise in Cardiovascular Health and Disease*, pp. 322–343. New York: Yorke Medical Books, 1977.

Anderson, P. The use of hand paddles, overload training, and after effects. *Swimming Technique*, 1976, 13(2):60–62.

Craig, A. B., Jr. Fallacies of hypoxic training in swimming. In J. Terauds and E. W. Bedingfield (eds.), *Swimming III*, pp. 235–239. Baltimore, Md.: University Park Press, 1979.

Dicker, S. G., Lofthus, G. K., Thornton, N. W., and Brooks, G. A. Respiratory and heart rate response to tethered controlled-frequency swimming. *Medicine and Science in Sports and Exercise*, 1980, 12:20–23.

Doherty, J. A. The effects of an interval training regimen on selected anthropometric measurements of female high school swimmers. Unpublished master's thesis, Ithaca College, 1977.

Frick, M., Konttinen, A., and Sarajag, S. Effects of physical training on circulation at rest and during exercise. *American Journal of Cardiology*, 1963, 12:142–147.

Luetkemeier, M. J. The effect of endurance swimming on the cardiorespiratory fitness levels of sedentary middle-aged men and women. Unpublished master's thesis, Ball State University, 1978.

Wilmore, J. H. Acute and chronic physiological responses to exercise. In E. A. Amsterdam, J. H. Wilmore, and A. N. DeMario (eds.), *Exercise in Cardiovascular Health and Disease,* pp. 267-273. New York: Yorke Medical Books, 1977.

Wilmore, J. H. Alterations in strength, body composition and anthropometric measurements consequent to a 10-week weight training program. *Medicine and Science in Sports and Exercise,* 1974, 6:133-138.

Woods, M. The effectiveness of an endurance swimming program on the physical fitness of college women as related to cardiovascular conditions, physique and motor fitness. Unpublished master's thesis, Greensboro Women's College, University of North Carolina, 1958.

Index